Jennifer Marshall Bleakley has done it again! These collected animal stories will find their way to your heart, just like the lovable creatures in the pages of this book. As you read, you'll laugh, you'll cry, and you'll say, "aww." Most importantly, you'll be reminded of just how much God cares for you. *Pawverbs* is an instant pick-me-up book that will delight readers everywhere.

RACHEL ANNE RIDGE, speaker, artist, and author of *Flash: The Homeless Donkey Who Taught Me About Life, Faith, and Second Chances* and *Walking with Henry: Big Lessons from a Little Donkey on Faith, Friendship, and Finding Your Path*

You and I have the privilege of reading this beautiful volume because Jennifer Bleakley loves Jesus. And loves animals. And, boy, can she write! These stories will generate some fabulous conversations.

MARGOT STARBUCK, author of *Small Things with Great Love: Adventures in Loving Your Neighbor*

I love how God uses creation and especially his creatures to teach us eternal truths. Jen Bleakley follows up her wonderful story of a blind horse named Joey with a book of animal-based proverbs that will warm your heart and instruct your soul.

DAVE BURCHETT, author of *Stay: Lessons My Dogs Taught Me about Life, Loss, and Grace*

Jennifer Bleakley's charming book brings together two of my favorite things: the antics of animals and the wisdom of Proverbs! *Pawverbs* warms your heart as it helps your faith. It's much more than a collection of stories about our furry friends; it's a thought-provoking journey through the book of Proverbs—and your own heart. Some stories bring a laugh; others draw a tear. Each anecdote springboards into a biblical lesson with practical applications to strengthen your faith. *Pawverbs* is the perfect devotional for animal lovers who love the Word of God!

ELIZABETH LAING THOMPSON, author of *When God Says, "Wait"* and *When God Says, "Go"*

Animals and nature are often irreplaceable in conveying the great mercy and faithfulness of the Lord when humans fail us. This tender collection of real-life animal stories takes "creature comforts" to a whole new level. I laughed, I cried, and I discovered renewed assurance of God's goodness demonstrated through the sweet beasts he has given us. He created this incredible diversity of creatures because he knew we needed their companionship—and what a gift they are! *Pawverbs* is a must-have addition to every animal lover's library.

AMY K. SORRELLS, author of *Before I Saw You*

Reading *Pawverbs* was the cold drink for which my world-weary soul thirsted. Breaking through division and disheartening news cycles, Jen Bleakley brings us the refreshing stories of our loyal furry friends. At first, I was skeptical that she could tie these sweet stories into Scripture, but I was wrong. Each tale (of tails!) holds a powerful truth, often bringing me to tears as I applied it to my personal life.

AMY CARROLL, Proverbs 31 Ministries speaker and writer, author of *Breaking Up with Perfect: Kiss Perfection Good-Bye and Embrace the Joy God Has in Store for You* and *Exhale: Lose Who You're Not, Love Who You Are, Live Your One Life Well*

Pawverbs

100 inspirations to delight an animal lover's heart

JENNIFER MARSHALL BLEAKLEY

TYNDALE
MOMENTUM®

The Tyndale nonfiction imprint

Visit Tyndale online at www.tyndale.com.

Visit Tyndale Momentum online at www.tyndalemomentum.com.

TYNDALE, Tyndale's quill logo, *Tyndale Momentum*, and the Tyndale Momentum logo are registered trademarks of Tyndale House Publishers. Tyndale Momentum is the nonfiction imprint of Tyndale House Publishers, Carol Stream, Illinois.

Pawverbs: 100 Inspirations to Delight an Animal Lover's Heart

Designed by Ron C. Kaufmann

Edited by Bonne Steffen

Published in association with Jessica Kirkland and the literary agency of Kirkland Media Management, LLC.

For information about special discounts for bulk purchases, please contact Tyndale House Publishers at csresponse@ tyndale.com, or call 1-800-323-9400.

ISBN 978-1-4964-4105-8

Printed in the United States of America

26	25	24	23	22	21	20
7	6	5	4	3	2	1

For Darrell, who always believes
I can do more than I think I can.
I love you more than words could ever say.

And for Sunny, Samson, Chief, and Bailey, four of the
greatest animals to ever grace this planet. Your time with us
was far too short, but the love you gave us and the lessons you
taught us will live on in the pages of this book
and in my heart forever.

Introduction

THROUGHOUT MY CHILDHOOD I had a menagerie of pets—rabbits, outdoor cats, goldfish, and even a grasshopper named Georgie. And while I desperately wanted a dog, I was never able to talk my parents into getting one.

As a painfully shy child, I often found it easier to connect with animals than I did with people.

Animals felt safer.

They didn't expect anything from me, and I didn't have to worry about what I said or what I looked like around them. They just offered the simple gift of companionship without the burden of my having to try to be someone I was not.

My pets were my very best friends and the keepers of all my secrets. But they were more than just my companions. In many ways, my pets became some of my greatest teachers. They've illustrated the importance of being present and listening; showed me what loyalty and trustworthiness look like; and helped me find my voice and be brave enough to share it.

While writing my first book, *Joey*, the true story of a blind horse who became an effective and inspiring therapy horse, I became acutely aware of the special connection people can form with animals.

Many people have discovered the blessings and benefits animals can bring to humans.

I think one of God's greatest kindnesses to us was filling this planet with animals—who can't talk, or post on the internet, or roll their eyes—but who are willing to just sit with us and be a friend.

But even more than offering us companionship, I believe God has given us animals, ultimately, to point us to himself—to the one who promises to never leave us. He loves us more than we can fathom and offers us peace, strength, joy, and hope.

I've become convinced that animals can be tangible manifestations of God's grace—whether they have paws, claws, or hooves! These fuzzy, furry, scaly, and feathery ambassadors point us to him and teach us how to live a life of joy.

The idea of animals being our teachers was the inspiration behind this book. *Pawverbs* is a collection of a hundred short stories, each one featuring a real-life animal and tying it to a principle or lesson from the book of Proverbs.

Several of the stories and photos in *Pawverbs* are of pets I've had throughout the years. But most were submitted by friends, family, coworkers, and even strangers who now feel like family.

And while each story is true, some happened a long time ago and were written from collected memories; others have had names and identifying details changed for privacy; and a few timelines have been adjusted for a more cohesive narrative. But the heart and integrity of the stories are all based on actual events.

Remember how I said I could never convince my parents to get a dog when I was growing up? Well, after getting married, I finally got a dog—in fact, we've had three Golden retrievers in our family over the years. Gracie is our most recent Golden girl and her antics have been a rich source of material.

At the end of each story, you will find a "Paws & Ponder . . ." and a "Paws & Pray" to prompt you to go deeper into the story and see a spiritual truth that might impact your own heart.

This was actually my biggest takeaway as I wrote this book—the realization that oftentimes the divine is hiding in the midst of the mundane.

Each day, I ask God to help me see things as they are, not as they appear to be. And my own pets—Gracie, a cat named Foxy, a bearded dragon named Captain Tim, and a beta fish named Barry—have been great teachers in helping me "paws" and pay attention so I don't miss a glimpse of our Creator.

Pawverbs brought such peace and joy to my soul when I was writing it, and I pray it will do the same for you as you read it.

With love,
Jen

Fear the LORD and shun evil. This will bring health
to your body and nourishment to your bones.

PROVERBS 3:7-8, NIV

1

AN ITCHY LESSON

Do not be wise in your own eyes; fear the Lord and shun evil.

This will bring health to your body and nourishment to your bones.

PROVERBS 3:7-8, NIV

THE DOG SCRATCHED and nibbled at her belly.

"Mom, Luna's chewing at herself again," ten-year-old Haley reported.

Angie looked at the inflamed, crusty sores on their chocolate Lab and knew it was time to make an appointment with the vet. She also knew how much Luna dreaded a trip to the vet. It always turned the normally happy-go-lucky two-year-old dog into a terrified, shaking scaredy-cat.

After dragging the trembling sixty-five-pound canine into the vet clinic, Angie sat with her dog in the exam room, awaiting the doctor's diagnosis.

"Allergies. Most likely a food allergy."

Angie had been plagued by allergies her entire life, so she empathized with Luna's suffering. She laughed at the coincidence. "Well, leave it to me to have a dog with allergies!"

The vet sent Angie and Luna home with antibiotics, anti-itch tablets, and a low-allergy food, and after a few days Luna's sores quickly healed. But they needed to pinpoint the source of the allergy through a process of elimination. So he put Luna on a strict diet to cleanse her system. Then, they reintroduced foods one by one. When Angie gave Luna a bit of chicken after a month into the process, the Lab started scratching again.

"I think we've found the culprit," the vet said, handing Angie a new prescription for anti-itch tablets. "No more chicken for you, Miss Luna."

Once the medicine took effect, the tender spots disappeared, and Luna was itch-free—for a few weeks.

Then Angie noticed welts on Luna's belly again.

"I just don't understand," Angie lamented to her husband. "She hasn't had an ounce of chicken. I feed her myself, and I know the kids haven't given her anything." After all, she had warned them. If they gave Luna any chicken, they would be paying for the next vet visit.

"Maybe she's allergic to something besides chicken," her husband suggested.

Angie opened the patio door for Luna as she continued to contemplate the situation. Instead of taking an immediate right toward the steps leading to the yard, Luna bounded to the left, where Georgia, the cat, was finishing her dinner on the patio table. Before Angie could react, Luna jumped up like a kangaroo, swiped at the stainless steel food bowl, and devoured the rest of the cat's dinner—looking oh so pleased with herself when she finished.

"When did she start doing that?" Angie wondered aloud as she raced after Luna.

Walking back into the house, she picked up the can of cat food she had opened that day for Georgia's dinner. *Creamy Delights: Chicken Feast.*

The cat food! No one ever thought to check the cat's food.

Of course, no one realized Luna had acquired kangaroo skills either.

With the mystery solved, Angie decided to move the cat's bowls into the garage, near the little cat door. She also figured it couldn't hurt to keep the cat on a chicken-free diet too, just in case Luna figured out how to start opening garage doors!

PAWS & PONDER...

When have you relied on your own wisdom instead of trusting in God's? What was the result? What cravings do you need to submit to God? How might things be different if you were to choose to trust God's way over your own?

Paws & Pray

Lord, so often I think I know best and choose my own way over yours. I confess that I crave things that ultimately harm me. Please forgive me and help me to trust you more. Help me to see you as you truly are: the almighty God—holy, righteous, loving, and good. Enable me to turn away from sin and turn toward you.

2

CAN'T WE ALL JUST GET ALONG?

When people's lives please the Lord, even their

enemies are at peace with them.

PROVERBS 16:7

"NO MA'AM!" Jessica yelled, as she walked into the family room. Their beagle, Emma, was using the family's new cat, Carey, as a chew toy. "We do not eat our friends!"

Jessica tightly held Emma by the collar as Carey bolted down the hall. Emma lunged forward, clearly wanting to give chase.

"Oh no, you don't, missy," Jessica chastised. "You are going to leave that cat alone and be nice!"

Ever since the family had adopted the sweet-natured cat in need of a home, their beagle had become obsessed with getting rid of her. Emma barked at Carey, chased her, stole her food, grabbed her by the neck, and had recently begun chewing Carey's tail while the poor cat hissed and scratched in protest. Jessica was done with Emma's behavior. Surely, a dog and a cat could share a home peacefully.

It was time to begin training Emma in earnest. Jessica taught her the "leave it" command—which applied to the cat, her food, and the litter box. She also taught Emma to lie on a particular cushion in the family room, on the opposite side of the room from the cat's bed. In addition to rewarding Emma when she responded to the new commands, Jessica also gave her a piece of kibble every time the cat entered a room, training Emma to run to her human instead of the cat.

"Good girl, Emma!" Jessica praised her dog one morning, several weeks into their new training. Emma had walked right by a sleeping Carey, without so much as a sniff in her direction. And the night before, when the family had piled on the sofa to watch a movie together, Emma had curled up with Jessica's daughter, Laci, while Carey had snuggled with her sons, Leyton and Seth.

After praising Emma, Jessica walked into the kitchen to pour herself a cup of French roast coffee, relishing a few tranquil moments. She inhaled the aroma of her coffee and soaked in the quiet peaceful morning.

"Mom!" Laci shouted from upstairs. "Leyton won't get out of the bathroom, and I *have* to get ready!"

Jessica heard her daughter pounding on the door.

"I'm not done! Hold your horses!" Leyton yelled through the door.

More pounding.

Jessica looked at Emma and Carey, now lying less than five feet from each other.

Wonder if some kibble treats would work on my kids too? she thought with a sigh.

PAWS & PONDER...

Living peacefully with the cat did not come naturally for Emma, the beagle. It required training. How might this truth apply to your life? How can you train yourself to better hear God's voice and obey his commands? Is there someone you are struggling to get along with and need God's help for a peaceful solution?

Paws & Pray

Lord, train me to hear your voice and obey your commands. I realize that humility and sacrifice are essential qualities for living a life of peace, but they do not come naturally to me. Help me to live in a way that pleases you. Let your peace fill me and then be extended to those around me.

3

WHERE'S PLUTO?

Smiling faces make you happy, and good news makes you feel better.

PROVERBS 15:30, GNT

"PLUTO'S GONE!" John shouted with panic in his eyes. "Ana, where is Pluto?!"

The teenage siblings were on the deck, cleaning the tank their leopard geckos shared. John had put his gecko in a temporary enclosure—a plastic food container with a partially secured lid—but now he was gone.

"He's a six-inch-long reptile, John," his older sister said, glancing to make sure her gecko was still in its temporary container. "He couldn't have gotten too far."

Her words were not calming. John frantically searched the deck, then he ran down the small set of stairs to peer under the deck. All he could see were piles of leaves, rocks of various shapes and sizes, cast-off gardening tools, and an old wheelbarrow.

"Should we get Coco to search for him?" Ana asked.

John's stomach lurched at the suggestion. He didn't want their eighty-pound German shepherd finding and gobbling his small gecko.

"No!" John shouted.

Hearing the commotion, John and Ana's parents joined the missing gecko search party. But after hours of searching every inch of the yard and house, the search party was called off.

Pluto was cold-blooded and needed heat—he had never been without his heat lamp.

John was heartbroken.

He loved his little reptilian friend and hated the idea of his spotted buddy alone and cold. And he couldn't even let himself think about his gecko becoming a meal for some hungry creature foraging at night.

Day after day John would go out with a flashlight and look for Pluto under the deck, hoping for any sign of his gecko. Temperatures were dropping into the low forties at night, the rain had been relentless, and a fox had been seen on their home security cameras several nights in a row. There was no way his pet could still be alive.

Eventually John resigned himself to the fact that Pluto, the world's greatest leopard gecko, was truly gone.

But then, three months after Pluto disappeared, John received a call from friends who lived in his neighborhood. They had seen a post on a neighborhood app about someone finding a strange spotted lizard in their garage. The person was asking if anyone knew what kind of lizard it was and what they should do with it.

John's friends took a screenshot of the lizard in question and sent it to him.

"That's Pluto!" John shouted into the phone. "That's *my* strange spotted lizard!"

After contacting the family who had found the lizard, John and his parents went to retrieve Pluto—almost a mile away!

Somehow John's little gecko had managed to safely cross a busy neighborhood street, meander through wooded areas and private yards, safely avoid hungry predators, and find his way into a garage in the middle of a heavy rainstorm.

John took Pluto home, placed him safely inside his tank, and secured the lid—checking it twice.

"Pluto, what an adventure you have had," John said as he admired his tough gecko. "But from now on, I think I'm gonna clean your tank . . . inside the house!"

PAWS & PONDER . . .

What good news have you received recently? How did that news make you feel? The word *gospel* is often translated as "Good News." What makes the gospel message—the life, death, and resurrection of Jesus Christ—such good news? How could you share that life-changing Good News with someone today?

Paws & Pray

God, your Word is full of good news—from your own lips declaring your Creation good, to your angel messengers heralding your good news to others when Jesus was born, to the life-changing good news of the gospel. Father, help me to share your Good News with others and to be generous in sharing what you have done in my life. Let my demeanor reflect the transforming power of the gospel.

4

A JOB FOR PEPPER

Laziness leads to poverty; hard work makes you rich.

PROVERBS 10:4, CEV

PEPPER LOVED TO WORK. From the moment the black and gray Australian shepherd awoke in the morning, she had one important mission—retrieve the paper. Pepper took her job very seriously.

So seriously, in fact, that some Sundays when the paper was too thick and heavy to fit in her mouth, Pepper would push it toward the house with her nose. Her owners, Kathy and Mike, were both amused and inspired by her persistence.

One Sunday, the newspaper had landed partly in some bushes near the driveway, making it impossible for Pepper to push it with her nose. She dug at the paper, frantically trying to grab it. When Kathy noticed Pepper's predicament, she went outside to help.

"That's okay, girl," Kathy said, collecting the newspaper. "I'll get it today."

Kathy turned to walk back to the house, but Pepper didn't move.

The dog sat at attention—head cocked to the side, ears up, eyes focused on the paper in Kathy's hands.

"Come on, Pepper," Kathy called. "Let's go inside."

But Pepper remained motionless, still staring at the paper.

Impressed by the commitment her dog had to her job, Kathy slid the paper from the plastic sleeve, pulled out the city/state news section, and handed it over.

Kathy chuckled as Pepper proudly carried her section of the paper into the house. Granted, large areas were illegible smudges because of Pepper's drool. But the Aussie was proud of herself. She had been trained for a job, and she took pleasure in completing that job every day.

With the delivery completed, Pepper devoured a bowl of kibble, spent some time in the backyard, and enjoyed a belly rub before falling asleep at Kathy's feet—likely dreaming of thinner papers tossed in open areas.

As Kathy read the paper, her gaze kept drifting to Pepper. She couldn't help but be convicted.

"God," Kathy prayed, "make me more like my dog—eager and happy to do the work you set before me. Give me the confidence and perseverance to complete each task. And if I can't, please send someone to help me."

Still sleeping, Pepper let out a series of muffled yips that sounded like chuckles.

"And yes, Lord," Kathy added with her own laugh, "if you send someone to help me, I promise I will still do my part and carry my own section."

PAWS & PONDER...

How do you feel about work? Do you think today's proverb is referring only to monetary riches as a reward for hard work? What other kinds of riches might this verse be addressing? Is there a task God has given you that you haven't started? What is holding you back? Would you make a commitment to him right now to complete that task as an act of worship and love?

Paws & Pray

Lord, some days I am discouraged at work. Please help me see that no matter what I do, it is work that you have given me to do. If I need assistance, let me set aside my pride and seek it. I want to approach each task as an act of love and worship. Show me how to find that balance between hard work and rest that you desire for my well-being.

5

SCRAM

The glory of the young is their strength; the gray hair
of experience is the splendor of the old.

PROVERBS 20:29

NO ONE REMEMBERS the little red dachshund's actual name. But from the moment three-year-old Caroline put her hands on her hips and called *scram*—the word she most associated with the dog who was always getting underfoot—the name stuck.

And Caroline's affection for him did too.

In many ways the tough little dog served as an anchor for Caroline through the ups and downs of her childhood. Her dog's tenacity, strong will, and ability to overcome any challenge inspired Caroline to get back up every time life knocked her down.

When Scram was hit by a car and survived, five-year-old Caroline knew she could get through her parents' divorce.

When Scram was attacked by a larger dog and his wounds eventually healed, Caroline believed that the wounds on her heart might one day heal as well.

And when Scram recovered from heartworm, which nearly took his life, Caroline knew she could recover when she had to leave her little friend behind as she moved with her mother to a new house.

The little dachshund went to live with her grandpa Alton. Caroline was glad she would still get to see Scram, but she was heartbroken that it wouldn't be every day.

She quickly realized, however, that her grandpa needed Scram just as much as she had.

Grandpa Alton loved Scram. He called him his little buddy, and the two were virtually inseparable.

As Scram aged, his slower pace was perfectly suited for Grandpa Alton. The two would sit together for hours on the back porch, nap together in Grandpa's favorite chair, and watch TV together every night.

And when Grandpa Alton felt like a short walk, Scram was always happy to accompany him.

The two were perfectly suited for each other.

When Scram died, Grandpa Alton cried for hours before burying his buddy in the backyard and marking his grave with a cross.

Over time Grandpa Alton's grief lessened, and he lived several happy years—although he never did get another dog.

Eventually, Grandpa Alton got sick, and his family knew his time on earth was coming to an end. Caroline came over one day, and her grandpa told her about a dream he had.

"I heard scratching at the back door, and when I opened the door, there was Scram! He looked at me, barked, and then started to walk away."

Tears rolled down his cheeks. "I know it won't be long now. Scram made me feel it was okay for me to leave all of you."

Grandpa Alton died a month later.

Caroline was so glad that Scram had been there for her grandpa, just like he had been there for her when she was a little girl.

Two lives were forever touched by the life of one special dog.

PAWS & PONDER...

Who has influenced your life from childhood to adulthood? In what ways have they influenced you? What benefits might come from friendships between young and old?

Paws & Pray

Father, thank you for everyone you have put in my life, especially people who are younger and older than I am. I value their gifts, which are different from mine. Together, we can use those gifts to support and help each other.

The prudent see danger and take refuge.

PROVERBS 27:12, NIV

6

ℋEARTFELT ℭOUNSEL

The heartfelt counsel of a friend is as sweet as perfume and incense.

PROVERBS 27:9

A WAVE OF PANIC rushed over Carol as she merged onto the interstate heading east out of Colorado—away from the state she had called home for seven years and the secure teaching job she had held since finishing grad school. *What am I doing?* she thought as she steered her small Mitsubishi Eclipse, packed full of boxes and suitcases, into the middle lane of traffic—squeezed between a large SUV and an even larger semi-truck. *Is this a rash decision?*

Mee-ooww!

Carol's one-year-old cat, Guinevere, had not stopped crying since being unceremoniously placed into a brand-new cat carrier and secured into the passenger seat.

"I know, sweetie. I know. This is scary for you," Carol said, keeping her voice soothing. "For whatever it's worth, it's scary for me, too."

Still, Guinevere continued to cry, sounding more pitiful with each mile.

"Sweetie, I promise to get you out of there soon. Just let me get through Denver, okay?" Carol placed her right hand against the front of the carrier. "Then it's wide open road and maybe you can come out."

The bumper-to-bumper traffic gave Carol plenty of time to reflect out loud. She was glad that someone was there to listen.

"Gwen, I had a good job. Sure, I wasn't happy . . ." Guinevere responded with a low groan that gave Carol pause. "Okay, okay, you're right, I was miserable. But it was a job with a steady paycheck. And I just walked away from it to pursue this crazy idea of getting into publishing. Who does that? And what if it doesn't work? What if this job at the newspaper isn't the step into publishing I think it could be? What if I end up being stuck as an entry-level beat reporter forever? What if I have to start sharing your Fancy Feast meals? What if . . ."

Wrraaoo.

Carol was startled by the primal sound erupting from her cat and nearly swerved into the other lane. Gwen had never done that before. Once again, Carol reached over and put her hand on the carrier to try to comfort her companion. As she glanced in the rearview mirror, she realized how far they had come.

"Well, look at that," she said in surprise. "We made it through Denver. Okay, Gwennie, I'm going to let you out of there. But don't freak me out. If you jump on the floor by my feet and the car pedals, we could get in an accident."

Guinevere shot out of the carrier the moment the latch was released and curled up in Carol's lap. Carol stroked her gently and continued to assure her trembling cat.

"Gwen, this is going to be an adventure for us. You're going to love Illinois, I promise. It's where I grew up and it's the best. You're going to be surrounded by so many people who love you."

Guinevere's trembling diminished to a slight quiver.

Carol continued, "And wait till you see the colors in the fall. Yes, the aspens in Colorado are pretty, but in Illinois the trees turn red, purple, orange, and yellow. It's incredible! And oh!" she shouted in excitement, causing Guinevere to jump. "Sorry, baby, but I just thought about your goopy eye. Remember how the vet said your eye would do better with more humidity? Well guess what Illinois has lots of? Humidity! I bet your eye is going to feel so much better!"

Carol felt Guinevere calm down with a resonant purr.

"We are going to get to play together and Mommy will pursue her dream job. Everything will work out, sweetie."

Realistically, Carol knew there would be difficult days ahead, and she still felt a little anxious about all the unknowns, but the more she talked to Guinevere, the more she began to believe her own words.

Fourteen hours later, Carol pulled into her parents' driveway exhausted from the long trip and yet at peace with her decision.

Holding Guinevere tightly in her arms, she walked to the front door. "No matter what the future holds, you and I are going to be just fine."

PAWS & PONDER . . .

Why do you think Carol's anxieties about her move were eased the more she talked to Guinevere? To whom do you turn when you need to talk things over or receive heartfelt counsel? What is some of the best counsel, or advice, you have ever been given? What made that counsel "sweet as perfume and incense"?

Paws & Pray

Father, thank you for being my wonderful Counselor and for always being there for me. Thank you for the people you have placed in my life who speak loving truth to me. And give me a passion for your Word so I can be a person who is willing and able to give wise and heartfelt counsel to others.

7

RING THE BELL

Listen to my instruction and be wise. Don't ignore it.

PROVERBS 8:33

CALLIE WAS ECSTATIC. Finally, after twenty-eight long years of waiting, she had her very own puppy—a brown Lab mix named Hershey. She picked up the nine-week-old puppy and snuggled him next to her face.

"I've waited so long for you, little one," she whispered. Before this moment, she had never felt her life was settled enough for such a responsibility, but now she felt fully prepared.

After finalizing the paperwork with the shelter, Callie secured Hershey in her car and took him home.

As soon as Hershey was old enough, Callie enrolled him in puppy school.

One evening, the instructor explained bell training—a method of potty training your dog by hanging a bell from the door knob and teaching the dog to ring the bell as a signal to go outside.

Callie was intrigued with the idea. She went home that night and hung a bell from a ribbon and attached it to the doorknob. At first Hershey was far more interested in playing with the bell. But Callie would ring it every time she opened the door to take him out. After a few days, she began using a treat to lure Hershey's nose to the bell, having him nudge it before opening the door.

Several weeks later, Callie was in the kitchen and heard a merry tingling sound. Hershey was standing by the door, nosing the bell to go out. "You are a genius, Hershey! Let me get your leash."

Hershey was rewarded with a trip outside and a handful of kibble treats.

From that day on, Hershey always rang his bell when he needed to go outside, and Callie always responded quickly to let him out.

When Hershey was two years old, Callie was upstairs working from home on a blustery day when she heard him ring his bell. She quickly got up and walked to the door, only to find Hershey with her slipper in his mouth.

"What are you doing, boy?" she asked, chuckling.

She opened the door, but Hershey didn't move.

Callie took a step toward her dog when suddenly he turned and ran into the family room, Callie in pursuit.

"Hershey, what has gotten into you?" she said, removing her slipper from his mouth.

Callie went back upstairs.

A few minutes later, Hershey rang the bell again. This time when Callie got to the stair landing, she saw Hershey standing at the bottom of the stairs with a water bottle in his mouth.

"Hershey!" she scolded. "Drop it."

When she took the first step down, Hershey took it as his cue to bolt. Hershey sprinted through the house, with Callie on his heels.

Three times around the sofa they went, and Callie had to stop.

She collapsed on the sofa and laughed.

"You little stinker! I guess you decided to train me on the bell too, huh? *Ring the bell and make Mommy chase me!* You really are a smart and silly dog."

Hershey thumped his tail in agreement.

PAWS & PONDER...

How does listening to God's instruction make a person wise? Have you been ignoring an instruction from the Lord? What is keeping you from obeying? Are you willing to take a step of obedience today?

Paws & Pray

Father, you are so wise. Forgive me for the times I choose not to listen to you. I love you and want to obey you. Keep giving me examples that I can learn from. Open my eyes and help me realize these are ways you show how much you care.

8

ĐEER SNOW WHITE

Ears that hear and eyes that see—the Lord has made them both.

PROVERBS 20:12, NIV

STACY OFTEN FELT as though she didn't belong.

Where her siblings were energetic and loud, she was reserved and quiet.

While her friends loved a good party, she preferred to stay home and read.

And where acquaintances engaged in small talk with ease, she found it tedious and painful.

"She's a square peg in a round hole," she had overheard others say. Eventually she began to believe them.

"All I want to do is blend into the background like wallpaper," the seventeen-year-old wrote in her journal one fall evening. "Instead, I seem to walk around like a neon sign blinking the words, Does not belong."

As she went to close the bedroom curtains, a flash of white caught her eye.

A white deer.

She had heard neighbors talk about spotting the rare white doe from time to time, but she had never personally seen it—until now.

She pressed her face against the cool window glass. The white doe grazed among a trio of more camouflaged deer. Stacy had to squint to see their brown coats in the diminishing light. But the white deer stood out like a beacon against the darkness.

Beautiful in its own right, but much like the ugly duckling in her favorite childhood book, it just didn't quite seem to belong.

As Stacy watched the white deer pull a dogwood leaf from a low-hanging branch, she identified with this rare animal that stood in stark contrast to the rest of the herd.

Day after day Stacy searched for the white deer. But as fall turned to winter and the Christmas lights got packed away for another year, she feared she would never see the elusive creature again.

But on a January morning, Stacy woke up and looked out the window. Snow was coming down so fast that she could barely see in the blizzard.

As her siblings put on winter gear and ran out the front door to start snowball fights in the front yard, Stacy went downstairs and sat in the family room, overlooking the much quieter backyard. She pulled a blanket around her shoulders and watched as the snow transformed the landscape.

Suddenly, Stacy saw a whirl of activity out of the corner of her eye.

Five deer dashed through the backyard, undoubtedly fleeing Stacy's rambunctious siblings. Four large brown deer bounded toward the back of the two-acre lot. But trailing behind the rest—taking her sweet time—was the white one.

Her pristine coat was now perfectly camouflaged in the snow—as if she had been born for this moment.

Tears formed in Stacy's eyes as she observed the white deer standing regally among the falling flakes. She was a snow queen observing her kingdom.

No longer did the doe look out of place.

No longer did she look like a square peg in a round hole.

She belonged here.

Her beauty and uniqueness were obvious—and breathtaking.

"You aren't a mistake," Stacy whispered. "You are beautiful and perfect and exquisite."

Stacy smiled as the doe leaped and ran with abandon before rejoining the herd. As the deer walked deep into the woods, Stacy realized that while the white doe was different, her difference was what made her beautiful, what made her special.

"Maybe that's true for me, too," Stacy said, grateful for the deer's visual affirmation.

PAWS & PONDER...

Have you ever struggled with feelings of not belonging? How did you deal with those feelings? Today's proverb says that God created a person's physical hearing and sight, but he gives us spiritual hearing and sight as well. How does knowing God created you a certain way—your appearance, personality, and talents—affect your sense of identity?

Paws & Pray

Father, I often feel alone and out of place. I fear that I simply do not belong anywhere. During those times, please open my ears and eyes to receive your truth. You created me, you love me, and you have a plan for me. Help me to trust your plan and your will for my life. Lord, when I struggle with feelings of isolation and loneliness, remind me who I am in you.

9

𝒜 HERO FOR PANDY

The righteous care for the needs of their animals,

but the kindest acts of the wicked are cruel.

PROVERBS 12:10, NIV

BRENDA WOULD NEVER call herself a hero. She's far too humble and unassuming to give herself such a title. However, if the numerous animals she has rescued over the years could talk, they would declare Brenda their hero, their champion, their friend.

Never meeting an animal she couldn't find room in her heart to love, Brenda has provided refuge and hope to many creatures throughout her life. And while she has loved them all, one particular dog—a black and white stray named Pandy—exemplified the lengths to which Brenda has gone to show love and kindness to an animal in need.

Pandy's plight began when his owners moved out of the house they rented from Brenda's father-in-law and left Pandy tied to a tree with a long chain. The owners left a bag of dog food with a neighbor and said they would return for Pandy.

They never did.

Brenda already had three dogs, two of whom were strays that Brenda had brought home. She knew if she met Pandy in person she would get attached and want to keep him. So Brenda's husband went by every day to feed the dog while Brenda tried to find a home for him. As much as they hated to leave Pandy outside, they decided it was the safest place for him while they continued searching for someone to take the abandoned dog.

Every call Brenda made was a dead end, so Pandy's only option was the SPCA (the Society for the Prevention of Cruelty to Animals). But even they couldn't take him for three weeks.

While they waited for an opening at SPCA, Brenda's husband continued to feed Pandy. But when his job began requiring him to put in longer hours, Brenda had to take over.

The more time she spent with the dog—who really did resemble a panda bear—the more she knew he deserved a home.

Finally, the SPCA called, and Pandy was treated for heartworm. But his stay was brief because Brenda couldn't imagine life without Pandy.

She brought him home, and he adjusted surprisingly well to his new environment and canine friends: Shack, Tippy, and Angel. Pandy was not as overtly affectionate as the other dogs, but Brenda could tell he was happy to have a real home. The quiet confidence he exuded warmed Brenda's heart, making her glad that the formerly abandoned dog felt a sense of assurance that Brenda would care for him.

Even when that care required costly surgeries.

Pandy suffered a broken leg—although no one knew how he broke it. Then years later, he was hit by a car and sustained a fractured back and head injury.

Brenda's husband joked he was going to make both Pandy and Brenda leave if the accident-prone dog kept requiring emergency vet services.

But Brenda knew he was teasing—he cared about Pandy as much as she did.

As Pandy's age and injuries kept him indoors more and more, Brenda regularly opened the door for him to gaze outside.

Sometimes he didn't even want to go out; he simply wanted to see outside—or maybe he just wanted to have the option to leave.

Brenda learned much from Pandy—things such as never giving up, never losing your willingness to trust, making the most of every day, and being willing to walk through an open door.

And Pandy learned what it meant to be loved, cared for, and championed.

PAWS & PONDER . . .

How do you define righteousness? Is there someone in your life you would describe as righteous? What character traits does this person have? How might today's verse also apply to our righteous God?

Paws & Pray

Father, thank you for how you care for me. Help me to care for others—including animals—out of the abundance of love you have for me. As I love and care for others, may I point them to you—the face of Love itself.

Eat honey, for it is good, and the honeycomb
is sweet to the taste.

PROVERBS 24:13

10

TWO LITTLE PIGGIES

Better to have little, with fear for the Lord,

than to have great treasure and inner turmoil.

PROVERBS 15:16

CAPTAIN CUDDLES and Lieutenant Nibbles were guinea pig sisters who became an Instagram hit thanks to their "mama" Mollie. Mollie had an impressive history with animals of various species and breeds, but she had never owned guinea pigs. And then she heard that the furry sisters needed a home.

Mollie was a creative person who loved to make cute things, so she was committed to making the piggies' lives over-the-top comfortable. Mollie bought a large cage and filled it with top-of-the-line bedding, tubes and tunnels where they could hide, and toys for them to play with. She filled her refrigerator with a smorgasbord of fruits and vegetables—a diet any piggie would envy. And to make her guinea pigs feel extra special, Mollie used her gifts with a needle and thread to sew blankets and decorative trinkets for them—and even a costume or two.

Mollie was overjoyed to bring her two little piggies home and wow them with their new goodies.

However, she quickly discovered that Captain Cuddles and Lieutenant Nibbles were rather indifferent to their guinea pig swag. They ignored the toys, rejected the tubes and tunnels, and burrowed under the fleece blanket after pushing it to the far end of the cage.

They just need time to adjust to their living quarters, Mollie thought.

So she waited. And waited. But still the two furballs seemed most content with the simplest of items—preferring an empty oatmeal container to their expensive Pig-loo and choosing to stay on their small fleece blanket rather than explore the expanse of the tiled floor in the kitchen.

As long as they had food, water, and a cozy place to snuggle, they were quite happy and content. Of course, from time to time they would make known a preference for or dislike of a particular food, but other than some diva-like behavior at mealtime, Captain Cuddles and Lieutenant Nibbles were two of the most contented animals Mollie had ever known—except when she decided to dress them up in costumes and share their photos on Instagram!

Thankfully they were willing to oblige Mollie with her guinea pig dress-up games. Perhaps they decided it was a small price to pay in order to enjoy the simple life they craved. A life they also shared with the family cat, Darcy, who they thought was their best friend—but who really was quite terrified of them! Still Mollie enticed Darcy to let the piggies play with her; after all, Mama couldn't crush their little guinea pig hearts. Providing two little guinea pigs with the simple life they wanted sure seemed to take an awful lot of work!

PAWS & PONDER...

What do you think of when you read the phrase *inner turmoil?* What kinds of inner turmoil can great riches or treasures bring? What does the phrase *fear for the Lord* mean to you? How does having awe and respect for God help you be grateful for what you have—even if it isn't much?

Paws & Pray

God, you alone are worthy of all of my worship and praise. No one is greater than you. Help me not to get so mired in my circumstances and troubles that I'm unable to see everything you've already done for me. I pray you'll make me content with what you have already provided. I desire to pursue you more than anything else.

11

TUCK'S BAD HABIT

You might learn their habits and not be able to change.

PROVERBS 22:25, GNT

JUDITH STRAIGHTENED THE SOFA pillows as her little dog, Tuck, gnawed on a bully stick in the kitchen. Grateful to have found something to keep him occupied, Judith finished speed cleaning. Tuck glanced at Judith every few minutes, sensing something was going on.

"Everything's fine, Tuck," Judith reassured her twelve-pound companion. "Nothing to worry about." But the fact was, she *was* nervous. Someone she hadn't seen in ten years was coming to visit. Although they had been best friends in high school, Judith was a different person now.

But she got the feeling Margo was exactly the same.

When Margo had called to say she would be in town for a few days and wanted to reconnect, Judith had been caught off guard. But she decided it would be rude to say anything but yes.

Margo interpreted that response to mean that Judith was inviting her to stay at her house for two nights. That wasn't exactly what Judith was saying, but she couldn't back out now.

After getting the last dish out of the dishwasher and putting it away, Judith scooped Tuck into her arms and kissed his fuzzy black head.

"I hope this goes okay," she said, burying her face in his fur. "Please be on your best behavior."

Tuck was Judith's protector. Although small in size, he was large in attitude to anyone he felt was a threat to Judith. His fierce loyalty warmed her heart but was worrisome at times, especially when her nieces and nephews—or possibly an old high school friend—came to visit.

Judith held Tuck tightly as the doorbell rang.

Tuck went berserk, barking and growling, struggling to get out of Judith's arms.

"Shh, Tuck. Quiet," Judith commanded.

Tuck squirmed out of her arms and ran to the door where he ramped up his barking to a ferocious level.

Judith got in front of Tuck as she opened the door. Margo looked—and smelled—exactly as Judith remembered. A blond model drenched in a cloud of cigarette smoke. Judith held her breath as she hugged her.

"Look at your little dog! What a funny-looking thing you are," Margo said, laughing at Tuck, who had quieted down when the door was opened.

Two days, Judith silently reminded herself.

"Let me show you the guest room," Judith said. "Oh, and please don't smoke in my house; I'm allergic. But you can smoke outside on the deck." Margo rolled her eyes but agreed.

When Margo was settled, she and Judith retreated to the deck. Tuck followed them outside, bringing his bully stick with him. He curled up on a chair cushion, with this bully stick clenched horizontally between his teeth.

Judith and Margo reminisced about high school days, old friends, and teenage escapades.

"So, is it true you found religion?" Margo eventually asked. "I heard from some mutual friends that you're a church girl now."

Judith briefly shared her story with Margo—how after a painful divorce she turned back to the God she had loved as a little girl but had wandered from as a teenager. She told Margo how the love of Jesus had healed the broken places inside of her and how much she loved her church family.

Margo teased Judith about her new Christian life. But Judith didn't mind. She loved her new life and the freedom she had found. And she silently prayed Margo would find it someday too.

As they talked, Margo lit cigarette after cigarette. Over the next two days, Margo spent more time outside than inside the house.

Judith was glad for the chance to reconnect with her childhood friend, and yet she breathed a sigh of relief when Margo left.

After throwing the guest room sheets in the laundry, Judith made a cup of tea and sat down to watch TV. She looked to see where Tuck was and nearly dropped her cup.

Tuck was lying on his dog bed holding the bully stick in his mouth like a long cigarette.

"Oh no, you don't, young man!" Judith said, grabbing the chew stick from his mouth.

Tuck tilted his head, confused at Judith's reaction.

"Sorry," she said sheepishly, handing it back to him. "It's been a long weekend."

Tuck took her offering and again gnawed on it as if it were a giant cigarette.

"Good grief, Tuck," Judith laughed, putting her cup down and grabbing his favorite ball. "How about we play ball for a bit? I'll try and help you kick your new habit before it gets out of control!"

PAWS & PONDER...

Have you ever picked up a bad habit from someone else? Were you able to overcome that habit? If so, how? While this proverb is often used as a warning against harmful behaviors, could it also be used to describe a positive behavior? What are some positive behaviors you could learn from others?

Paws & Pray

Lord, help me lead others closer to you. I want to be a bold witness for you. Convict me of any wrong behavior and thoughts I have. Help me to treasure your words and your ways. Father, forgive me of my sin, change my heart, and help me to walk with you.

1 2

GO LEFT

The prudent understand where they are going,
but fools deceive themselves.

PROVERBS 14:8

JUSTUS WAS ONLY A FEW MONTHS old the first time he saw a squirrel in his backyard climbing down a large oak tree.

The small yellow Lab, whose nose had been pressed to the ground as he explored his new surroundings, was startled by the sound of claws scratching against tree bark. Justus tilted his head, wagged his tail, and then he was off. Driven by both instinct and curiosity, Justus ran as fast as he could.

The squirrel stopped his descent, confident he was safe on the tree trunk several feet from the ground.

Justus barked and pawed the tree.

Desperate to play with this new and interesting friend, he play-bowed numerous times.

The squirrel was unimpressed and chattered noisily as he scampered farther up the trunk.

Confused and dejected, Justus stared at the tree for several minutes before lowering his nose and resuming his sniff patrol.

Day after day, the squirrel descended from its nest and Justus gave chase as it turned and scampered up the tree.

Squirrel quickly became Justus's favorite word. He would bark frantically at the mere mention of the creature who refused to come down for a proper hello.

As Justus grew from puppy to full-size dog, his interest in squirrels grew from curiosity to a full-blown obsession.

And yet, much to his owner, Will's, amusement, no matter where in the yard a squirrel was, Justus always, without fail, ran straight to the oak tree in the middle of the backyard.

"Justus, squirrel!" Will would shout, pointing to a squirrel on the fence opposite the oak tree.

Justus would bark and paw at the door. He would see the squirrel to his left, balancing on the top of the fence. But the minute the door opened, Justus would make a hard right and run straight to the oak tree.

One day, hearing a squirrel's distinct chattering, Justus bounded out the door, took his hard right, and then let out a yelp. He limped to the tree.

No squirrel there.

Forlorn at not nabbing the elusive squirrel, he limped back inside.

Will took his squirrel hunter to the vet, who revealed that Justus's enthusiastic chase had resulted in a torn ACL.

"Oh, Justus," Will whispered in his Lab's ear while he was being prepped for surgery. "Next time go left."

Justus recovered from surgery and lived many more happy years. But never once did he turn left.

PAWS & PONDER...

Has your enthusiasm for something ever caused you to run ahead of God—or miss his leading altogether? Maybe it was a relationship or an opportunity you pursued despite the Holy Spirit prompting you not to. How did that situation turn out? How can you guard yourself from making a mistake when enthusiasm swells in your heart?

Paws & Pray

Lord, so often I think I am going the right way in life, only to discover I've made a wrong turn. Help me to walk with you, Father—to go where you lead. Stop me from running ahead of your plans for me.

13

A TALE OF TWO DOGS

Let love and faithfulness never leave you; bind them around your neck, write them on the tablet of your heart. Then you will win favor and a good name in the sight of God and man.

PROVERBS 3:3-4, NIV

ONE LOYAL DOG. One former president. One heartwarming photo on the internet—and suddenly the entire country knew the name Sully, the service dog to late President George H. W. Bush. The image of the yellow Labrador retriever lying dutifully in front of his flag-draped coffin became the embodiment of loyalty and honor to a grieving nation.

The two-and-a-half-year-old service dog had done his job well. He had provided companionship, acts of service, and loyalty to the former president in his final months. Even after the president's death, Sully remained in his service and at his side. Loyalty and faithfulness—traits that can leave a lasting impression on others, even if no one captures a viral-worthy photo or the world is unaware of an animal's name or story.

Such was the case with Samson—a black Lab belonging to a woman named Judy.

While Samson may share a name with a rather infamous Bible hero, the world never had reason to know this dog's name.

Samson never served a president, nor aided a war veteran. And his humble act of service was never reported on the nightly news.

But the way Samson demonstrated loyalty and faithfulness to Judy's family makes him a hero in her eyes.

The midnight-colored Lab adored Judy's elderly parents, D. L. and Grace, whom he stayed with during the day when Judy worked.

Judy's dad would play ball with Samson for hours—oftentimes throwing the ball from a chair because the dog's endurance outmatched his own. If Samson wasn't playing catch with D. L., he was following him around like a shadow.

But then one day, D. L. became too sick to get out of bed. Thankfully, his "shadow" didn't seem to mind. Instead, Samson just climbed up next to him. As Judy and her mom, along with the hospice nurses, tried to make D. L. comfortable, Samson remained by his side in the bed.

Loyal and faithful.

Samson was with D. L. until he drew his last breath.

Then after taking a final sniff of his favorite ball thrower, Samson turned his attention to Grace and Judy.

He lay with Judy at night as she cried.

He sat with Grace each day as she mourned.

Samson's constant presence steadied both of them through the storm of grief and loss. The black Lab helped them find their way to a new normal.

He reminded them of sweet memories but also helped them build new ones.

Sully and Samson.

Two loyal dogs.

Two faithful companions.

Two very good names.

PAWS & PONDER . . .

Why are love and faithfulness so important in this world? Who would you consider a loyal and faithful person in your life? What do you want people to think about you when they hear your name?

Paws & Pray

Lord, you tell me in your Word that you will never leave me nor forsake me. Thank you for being the perfect example of love and faithfulness. Help me honor your name by following your lead and living my life in the same way.

14

THE VEST

Hard work will give you power; being lazy will make you a slave.

PROVERBS 12:24, GNT

"ARE YOU READY TO VISIT?" Sheila asked Baxter as she held up the blue vest embroidered with the words "Please pet me; I'm a therapy dog."

Baxter barked and jumped excitedly until Sheila said, "Vest." Immediately, the collie calmed down so Sheila could put the vest on him and attach a leash to his collar. Then they walked to the car for the short ride to the local hospital.

Sheila was always amazed at Baxter's transformation from a playful, even silly three-year-old dog at home, to a calm and focused therapy dog once he was in "uniform."

As soon as Baxter walked through the hospital doors, he instantly became attuned to the needs of those around him—seeking out people who were hurting or sad, sitting with others who were lonely, lying calmly beside those who were anxious.

His focus and determination on the job were admirable.

Sheila often joked with her friends that she needed to buy a work vest for her teenagers to get them as motivated to do their homework as Baxter was to visit patients.

Sheila loved walking through the hospital with Baxter, watching him do the work he clearly loved.

Baxter tried to greet everyone as he and Sheila walked through the halls—doctors, nurses, orderlies, and family members. Many times,

Baxter ministered to someone in the halls, long before he ever made it into a patient's room.

Sheila called it Baxter's "Spidey-Sense"—his uncanny ability to know exactly who needed a snuggle, a paw, or just someone to sit with. As Baxter sat with a scared family member or an overworked professional, Sheila got to witness firsthand the calming and reassuring effect her dog had on others.

And when Baxter walked into a patient's room, it was like seeing the sun break through dense cloud cover. Smiles abounded, spirits lifted, and sometimes tears flowed. Baxter did his job well.

Back at home, the vest came off, and Baxter burned off his remaining energy with a lively game of catch before falling into a deep sleep on his dog bed—which Sheila had embroidered with just one word: Hero.

PAWS & PONDER . . .

In what ways can hard work empower you? Conversely, how might laziness make you a slave? Why are we often resistant to hard work? What work has God given you to do today?

Paws & Pray

Father, thank you for the gifts of work and rest. You set the example for us to follow—for six days you created the universe and then rested on the seventh. Enable me to work hard at the things you have given me to do, and then help me to rest well.

Whoever is patient has great understanding.

PROVERBS 14:29, NIV

15

ḤAPPY'S GIRL

Whoever is patient has great understanding,

but one who is quick-tempered displays folly.

PROVERBS 14:29, NIV

MAKING FRIENDS WAS DIFFICULT for three-year-old Olivia, whose temporary hearing loss during a critical period of her development had left her unable to communicate like most of the other children her age.

Her mother, Jackie, wanted nothing more for her daughter than to experience the joys and giggles of a happy, normal childhood. And yet day after day Olivia seemed to pull further and further into her own silent world. Sadly, it was a world in which playdates with other children simply didn't exist.

But then Happy joined the family. The pit bull mix had a perpetual smile, and he became Olivia's closest friend—a very large, very patient, unlikely best friend who was always delighted to play with the little girl he adored.

Often judged solely on his size and the reputation of the breed he most resembled, Happy continually surprised people who took the time to get to know him. His blocky head and stocky body housed the sweetest temperament Jackie had ever known in a pet. It was the perfect temperament for playing with a three-year-old.

Jackie continually marveled at how calm, gentle, and patient Happy was with Olivia. He seemed to naturally understand her limitations, and he adapted to her communication style. A push against his side meant she wanted him to lie down, and a push against his rear meant he was to sit. Olivia had a distinct way to call him and he eagerly responded.

And yet, the thing that warmed Jackie's heart most was watching them play. Olivia would make Happy sit, place a tea cup in front of him, and proceed to have a tea party with him. Other times Olivia would give Happy the special command to lie down so she could give him a thorough checkup with her Fisher-Price doctor's kit. Her daughter never seemed to run out of ideas. Like the time she attached a laundry basket full of stuffed animals to Happy's collar with a scarf and giggled nonstop when he took her toys on a bouncy ride across the room.

Happy was the ideal playmate for Olivia. He provided the perfect balance of sensitivity, playfulness, and companionship she needed at that time of her life.

Eventually, Olivia's hearing was restored, thanks to ear tubes and medication to clear the fluid in her ears. She began making significant strides in her communication skills, giving her the ability to make friends.

And yet, Happy still remained her most trusted confidant and closest friend. He was the one who understood her when many others could not, and he played with her when many others would not.

His patience and gentleness created a childhood for Olivia that she will always remember with fondness and joy.

He was her Happy, and she was his girl.

PAWS & PONDER...

In what ways does understanding produce patience? What are some blessings you might miss if you are unwilling to be patient? What blessings did Olivia receive from Happy's patience with her? What are some blessings you have received when you were patient?

Paws & Pray

Lord, you are the all-knowing, all-understanding, and most patient God. Thank you for extending patience to me. Please help me be patient with others. And Lord, just as Happy restrained himself and allowed Olivia to lead, help me to show humility and understanding to others so that I might be a blessing and show them a glimpse of your love.

16

ꝒROP ꞮT!

Whoever guards his mouth preserves his life;

he who opens wide his lips comes to ruin.

PROVERBS 13:3, ESV

"DROP IT, JASPER!" Kelsey commanded her six-month-old puppy.

The Welsh corgi locked his jaws even tighter around his most recent find—a prickly seed capsule known as a sweet gum ball. It looked like a cross between a pine cone and a sandspur, and when the sweet gum trees dropped them in the fall, they were everywhere in the neighborhood. Jasper seemed determined to snag each and every one during their morning walk.

Actually, Jasper seemed determined to put most anything in his mouth—rocks, trash, clothing . . . even a dead turtle.

It was just a week prior that Jasper had devoured a decomposed turtle before Kelsey could react and get it out of his mouth. Not surprisingly, he got sick and began throwing up. After one ridiculously expensive trip to the emergency vet, Jasper was "grounded" indoors for several days without a walk.

But when he recovered and returned to his energetic little puppy self, Kelsey relented and decided to try another walk. Within minutes Jasper had sucked up the prickly seed ball.

"Ugh, Jasper, walking with you is like taking a vacuum cleaner for a stroll!"

Kelsey knelt down and attempted to pull open his mouth. She was able to separate Jasper's clenched jaws just enough to grasp the spiky ball and throw it out of Jasper's reach.

"Buddy," she said wearily, rubbing his soft head. "I'm just trying to keep you safe. You're going to get hurt again if you don't learn to keep your mouth closed." She rubbed her slobbered hand on her jeans. "And just so you know," she added, holding her index finger and thumb two inches apart. "I'm this close to making you wear a muzzle!"

Kelsey stood, looked up and down her quiet street, and then moved Jasper toward the middle of the road—away from the grassy shoulder that contained so many tempting treasures. Jasper pulled and tugged against his leash, but Kelsey kept him in line.

The next day she decided to take a pocket full of treats with her, hoping to keep Jasper's focus on the right thing to put in his mouth. It worked! The playful little puppy became much more interested in turkey jerky bits than roadside offerings.

Over the next several weeks, Kelsey worked on "drop it" and "leave it" commands at home. When Jasper obeyed, he was rewarded with a delicious morsel.

Six months later, when they were on their daily walk, Jasper found a piece of rotting fruit in the grass.

"Leave it," Kelsey said firmly. Jasper stopped and looked up.

"See, buddy," she said, as she gave him a treat and a good rub on his side. "Things go so much better for you when you learn to control that little mouth of yours."

PAWS & PONDER ...

Jasper had to learn to control what went into his mouth. Oftentimes, we need to learn to control what comes out of ours. Have your words ever gotten you into trouble? What could you have done differently in that situation? How can you train yourself to guard your mouth?

Paws & Pray

Lord, in your Word you compare a person's tongue both to rudders that steer ships and to sparks that start fires. Would you help me control my tongue and only speak the words you want me to say? It's so easy to get pulled into gossip and respond with negative words and insults on social media. Father, train me to stop and think of what I want to say. May mine be words of life, grace-filled truth, and love.

17

A CANINE RAP SHEET

When you tell the truth, justice is done, but lies lead to injustice.

PROVERBS 12:17, GNT

"PAUL, HAVE YOU SEEN Jack and Piper?" Jan asked.

"I let them out in the back yard."

Jan looked out the window. "Well, they're not there now."

The couple began searching the surrounding area, calling the black Labs' names. They drove around the neighborhood for blocks. When they got back home, they called friends and neighbors, asking them to be on the lookout for two canine escape artists that had somehow gotten past the fence.

"Is there anything else we can do?" Jan asked Paul. She was getting more anxious by the minute. "I don't want anything to happen to them."

"Let's wait a little while, and then we'll go out again."

A few minutes later, a police car pulled up in front of their house. The officer was flanked by two familiar dogs—Jack and Piper! Jan and Paul met them at the front door.

"I was on patrol when I noticed these two wandering around and guessed they belonged to someone," the officer said. "When I stopped the car, they ran up to me. They are certainly friendly dogs. I opened the back door of the car and they jumped in. We gave them water and snacks at the station, then checked their tags. I think they're glad to be home."

"Thank you so much," Jan said, scooting the two Labs inside. "I'm so glad you found them. We'll make sure it doesn't happen again."

The next time the canine pair set off on an adventure, Jan and Paul didn't even know they were gone. This time, Paul answered the door. It was a different police officer but the same guilty parties.

"I found the dogs running down the middle of the road," he said. "I took them to the station in the squad car and found out where they lived."

Paul thanked the gracious officer profusely and vowed he would seal the dogs' escape hatch in the fence.

Weeks passed without an incident. "I think we've solved the problem," Paul said to Jan with confidence. He had created a brick barrier at the bottom of the fence where the dogs had been digging.

A month later, Jan and Paul were having dinner when there was a rap on the door.

Guess who?

"You've got to be kidding me," Paul said, exasperated.

The officer with Jack and Piper chuckled, then said, "Yep, found them again. Although this time they came to us. Just ran right up to the front door of the station like they knew exactly where to go."

Jan was mortified—again—but couldn't help but laugh. Leave it to their dogs to turn themselves in to their new friends—the police!

For months to come, Jack and Piper got quite a rap sheet from playing their favorite game: escape to the police station. Thankfully, the officers didn't seem to mind.

PAWS & PONDER...

Just like Jack and Piper learned to run straight to the police station, God wants you to run to him when you sin. And just like the officers welcomed the dogs, God welcomes you even when you've run off on your own. Do you tend to run toward God or away from him when you have messed up? What dangers might you face when you attempt to hide your sin with lies and deception?

Paws & Pray

Father, help me to run toward you and not away from you when I sin. Give me courage to speak the truth, even when it's hard. Remind me how harmful it is when I try to cover up my sin with lies. Lord, help me not to stray from your path. Thank you for always welcoming me into your arms, no matter what I've done.

18

ᑌNDERSTANDING ᒪOLA

A person's thoughts are like water in a deep well,

but someone with insight can draw them out.

PROVERBS 20:5, GNT

FRUSTRATION SURGED THROUGH Bruce as he stared at his dog, Lola. The two-year-old border collie had been standing in the family room barking incessantly for the past five minutes.

"What?" Bruce bellowed, unable to take the sound anymore. "I took you outside. I fed you dinner. You've been for a walk. You had a treat. What else could you possibly want?"

Bruce's head was pounding, and Lola's psychotic barking was not helping.

Lola stopped momentarily as she listened to Bruce's tirade, then resumed the cacophony.

All Bruce wanted to do was lie on the sofa and watch a movie. His wife and kids were at a birthday party, and he was looking forward to a quiet evening—until Lola went berserk.

With his movie on pause and his popcorn still in the microwave, Bruce got on the floor next to Lola and looked around, trying to see from her vantage point.

"Okay, girl, I see no bad guys. I smell no smoke. And we don't have a well, so I know there's no kid named Timmy trapped inside of it. So, what is your deal?"

Lola flattened her body to the floor, turning her head toward the sofa. Bruce mimicked Lola's actions. And there, under the sofa, was Lola's favorite ball.

"Well, I'll be . . ." Bruce said, retrieving the ball for his dog. "Why didn't you just say your ball was stuck?" He laughed as he tossed the ball to Lola.

With her ball tucked safely in her mouth, Lola lay down on her bed, and Bruce finished watching the movie.

Several days later Bruce and Lola were alone again when she started her rhythmic barking—this time while standing by the kitchen island. Thinking she must have lost her ball again, Bruce scanned the room. Her ball was under the table. He tossed it to her. Lola didn't even try to catch it. She simply kept barking. Bruce texted his wife to make sure she had fed Lola that morning. She had.

Here we go again, he thought, trying to figure out why Lola seemed distressed.

What are the symptoms of mad cow disease? Can dogs get it? Bruce tried to ignore Lola and clean off the island counter before heading into work.

As he lifted a discarded dish towel, he discovered someone's breakfast plate—most likely his twelve-year-old son's, who had forgotten to put it away. And there on the plate was half a banana, which happened to be Lola's favorite fruit.

Bruce looked at his dog, who had suddenly gone quiet. Her gaze was fixed on the banana in his hand. Two ribbons of drool streamed from her mouth.

"What?" Bruce teased. "You want this ol' thing? This sweet, yummy banana?"

He pretended to take a bite before tossing it to Lola.

Over the next several weeks, Bruce became an expert at interpreting Lola's barks. Like a mother able to decipher her infant's cries, Bruce learned how to tell the difference between Lola's vocalizations.

At first he had been irritated by her barking, but after taking the time to try to understand her behavior, he realized her barks were a sign of her high intelligence. She was communicating with him. Whether letting him know the cat wanted to come in, or she needed help retrieving a toy, or asking for a chunk of ice, or for an invitation to sit with him on the sofa, Lola knew what she wanted and wasn't shy about asking.

All she needed from Bruce was a willingness to listen.

PAWS & PONDER...

So often a person gets stuck in "surface" conversation. You hear someone's words— or see her actions—but you don't take the time to look past the surface and try to understand what the other person is really trying to say. Why is it important to really listen and pay attention to those around you? What might happen today if you set aside your distractions and really listened and paid attention to someone? You might be surprised by what you learn.

Paws & Pray

Father, I'm guilty of not really seeing and hearing others. I don't want to be content with surface relationships and conversations; I desire to go deeper and really engage with others in a way that brings them life and hope. I need your help to be that caring individual.

19

GIDEON

A glad heart makes a happy face; a broken heart crushes the spirit.

PROVERBS 15:13

IF EVER A DOG WAS JUSTIFIED in being bitter about his life, it was Gideon.

He had lived the first year of his life as a stray. Then, barely a year old, he wandered into the wrong yard and was attacked by the resident's dogs. The kind owner of the dogs took the injured stray to the veterinarian to have his wounds treated. During the examination, the vet realized the puppy's back right leg was not working correctly.

After several X-rays, the vet determined that the friendly black puppy must have been hit by a car or sustained some other traumatic injury in his young life, and his leg had not healed properly.

Unable to repair the damage done to the dog's leg, and realizing the leg was a liability and hazard to the dog's well-being, the decision was made to amputate the limb. Following the surgery, the puppy—who had been named Gideon—was turned over to a local rescue organization to recuperate.

Eventually, he was adopted by a kind woman named Amy, who saw in Gideon not a grumpy dog, but a happy-go-lucky dog who was always ready to play.

Amy prayed Gideon would enjoy his new home with Finlea, her active year-old Golden retriever. Finlea was a great dog, but she clearly preferred humans to other canines. In fact, before Gideon walked through the door, Finlea had been nervous around every other dog she had ever met. However, the moment she and Gideon greeted each other, they bonded.

Finlea and Gideon loved to play together—chasing each other around the yard and wrestling together inside. Amy was delighted that Gideon was adjusting to his new home so quickly. And she was amazed by how easily he had adapted to life with three legs.

Gideon was the very definition of happiness. Even the little skip he had to his gait reflected his zeal for life.

Unfortunately, about a year after his adoption, on an icy day in January, Gideon tore his ACL in his remaining back leg. The vet said surgery would be impossible with Gideon's limitations and so the only option was intense rehab, a custom brace, and restricted access to the furniture and play. Amy worried how Gideon would handle such a huge setback. Would his jovial personality be affected forever?

And yet, even with all of the new challenges, Gideon remained the happy, face-licking, tail-wagging, sweet-natured dog he had always been. He took every obstacle in stride and was never bothered by what he couldn't do. Instead, Gideon simply pressed on with what he *could* do.

Gideon became Amy's inspiration during difficult days. Whenever she felt overwhelmed or started to have a pity party for herself, she would picture Gideon's happy expression and joyful disposition and remind herself that she needed to focus on the good and not dwell on the bad.

When Gideon fully recovered from his ACL injury, he continued to enjoy every moment of his life with Finlea by his side and a big canine smile on his face.

PAWS & PONDER...

How does a broken heart crush someone's spirit? Have you ever experienced a crushed spirit? What made your heart glad? Have you experienced God's healing presence in your life?

Paws & Pray

Lord, you are the source of true joy and contentment. I know I will always feel safe in your arms, but some days my spirit is so crushed, I can barely do anything. I need to see glimpses of your presence. Would you heal my broken heart and crushed spirit and fill my mind with an awareness of you? Let me rejoice in you. And help me to share that gladness with others.

Hope deferred makes the heart sick,

but a desire fulfilled is a tree of life.

PROVERBS 13:12, ESV

20

RULE FOLLOWER MEETS RULE BREAKER

Doing wrong is fun for a fool, but living wisely

brings pleasure to the sensible.

PROVERBS 10:23

MILLIE'S FAMILY OFTEN SAID that their highly sensitive Boston terrier was the world's most well-behaved dog. At the mature age of six, Millie had learned the family's routine, knew what they expected from her, and was always eager to please.

She was also very good at reading people's emotions and body language—so good, in fact, that it could sometimes be a problem. For example, if someone in the family got upset about something, Millie assumed they were upset with her. She would be overcome with imagined guilt and run away, curl into a little ball, and make herself as small as possible.

It often took a while to convince Millie to come out of her self-imposed time-out. But once she did, she quickly went back to her sweet-natured, obedient, docile self.

Millie's highly ordered and rule-following world was working just fine.

And then Moxie joined the family.

Moxie, a little kitten with a big penchant for trouble, blew into Millie's quiet ordered life like a tiny tornado—tossing mischief around like flying debris.

The first week Moxie was with them, she explored the house and found so many interesting things to play with—like the dial on the gas fireplace! With a flick of her curious paw, the fireplace turned on, reducing the decorative candles that were inside it to puddles of melted wax.

The black-and-gray-striped kitten upped her game by learning how to take stoppers out of bathroom sinks and bat small items—oftentimes earrings—down the drain.

The tiny prankster also developed a habit of hiding her family's possessions in secret nooks and crannies throughout the house.

Moxie's mischievous ways caused some frustration for her human family, but no one was more bothered by her antics than poor Millie—who grew more and more anxious from Moxie's blatant disregard for rules and order.

Millie would pace when Moxie was on the prowl for kitten-sized trouble. She would whine when Moxie seemed to find the trouble she was looking for. And the Boston terrier would run and hide the moment her humans would come home to discover a Moxie-sized mess.

The look of guilt on Millie's face made her owners chuckle.

"Oh, Millie girl, we know you didn't do it. You're okay," they would reassure the nervous dog.

Millie would lick and nuzzle her humans as if trying to apologize for Moxie's behavior.

And Moxie? She did not seem the least bit concerned by her family's frustration. Instead, she would sashay right by Millie—undoubtedly in search of another bauble to plink down a drain.

PAWS & PONDER ...

Did you see yourself as Millie or Moxie in this story? Have you ever done something foolish and actually enjoyed it—at least for a moment? In what ways can living wisely bring pleasure? Do you think that living wisely means never having any fun?

Paws & Pray

Lord, far too often I choose what is foolish, and yet I want to be wise. While the foolish choice can sometimes seem more fun, help me remember that true joy—lasting joy—is found in you. Help me to choose your way over my own and in doing so find pleasure for my soul and enduring joy.

21

WHERE'S BEAR?

The simple believe anything, but the prudent give thought to their steps.

PROVERBS 14:15, NIV

JODY BELIEVED HER DOG Molly, a two-year-old border collie/ Lab mix, was the smartest dog she had ever had. Molly had earned top honors when she completed puppy school and had quickly moved up the obedience school ladder, earning a Canine Good Citizen certificate well before her first birthday.

Molly had an impressive list of tricks she would run through whenever Jody's friends stopped by. And most impressive to Jody, Molly knew her left from her right and could find a specific toy when asked.

Molly's advanced intelligence amazed Jody. But it also amused her.

Jody had learned from Molly that you could be ridiculously smart and still be incredibly gullible.

Molly adored her best friend Bear—a big, gentle three-year-old Rottweiler who lived next door. The two were together almost every day. Any time Molly heard someone say Bear's name, she would run to the back door in anticipation of playing with her friend—regardless of the time of day or if she had just come in from seeing Bear.

Jody's kids used the "Bear card" when Molly had one of their socks in her mouth and they wanted her to let go.

"Where's Bear?" they would ask excitedly. And without fail, Molly would drop the sock in one of the kids' hands before racing toward the back door.

JENNIFER MARSHALL BLEAKLEY

Jody used the "Bear card" when she was trying to get work done at home and Molly started barking.

And Jody's husband used the "Bear card" when he wanted to enjoy a bowl of ice cream without Molly drooling all over his feet . . . because he found it amusing.

Sometimes Molly's humans felt a little guilty for tricking their gullible dog, but she didn't seem to mind.

After all, she may have been gullible, but she was smart enough to know that one of those times the back door would open and she would get to romp with Bear.

Wait! Did someone say Bear?

PAWS & PONDER . . .

What are the dangers of gullibility? Have you ever trusted the wrong person? What was the result? What role does discernment play in taking others at their word? What steps do you need to ponder today?

Paws & Pray

God, you are most trustworthy and good. Grant me the discernment I need to navigate relationships. Enable me, by your Spirit, to know who I can trust and who I cannot. Teach me to be a trustworthy person so I can point others to you.

22

ℱACE-PLANT

Pride leads to disgrace, but with humility comes wisdom.

PROVERBS 11:2

AFTER DUMPING THE CONTENTS of a large IKEA box into the middle of his family room, Darrell stood back and assessed the parts of the bookcase his wife had ordered lying scattered all over the floor.

Why didn't she just ask me to make her one? he wondered. *I certainly could do it.* After all, he could build most anything—headboards, dressers, cabinets, tables, even custom bookcases. Granted, with his full-time job as a software engineer, his turnaround time wasn't exactly expedient. But he enjoyed the creative outlet, and others seemed to enjoy what he made.

He had heard his wife declare that they needed more storage a few weeks earlier, then mumble something about needing it quickly. When nothing happened, she ordered the white Billy bookcase from IKEA.

Darrell glanced at the instructions in his hand before tossing it aside.

Who needs instructions? You simply lay out all the pieces, then put them all together.

Easy peasy.

As Darrell began laying out the side panels, something outside the bay window caught his eye.

Three squirrels were chasing each other up the trunk of the old oak tree in the middle of the yard. Darrell turned his attention to the chattering trio—hoping they wouldn't disturb the birdhouse and feeder he had secured to the tree the day before. It was the first project his kids had completed with only minimal help, and they were so proud of their accomplishments.

His daughter had decided on a classic style wooden birdhouse, while his son had chosen to construct a tray-style feeder—allowing the birds to stand on the side and eat freely from the open middle. When the birdhouse and feeder were completed, Darrell secured them to the oak tree. The birdhouse was attached to the trunk, while the feeder was suspended in midair between two branches in hopes of keeping the squirrels away. After adding birdseed to the feeder, Darrell and his kids stepped back to admire their work. Moments later, the kids squealed with delight as two robins flew straight to the tray feeder, helping themselves to a birdseed buffet, before investigating the round entry into the birdhouse.

But now, as Darrell watched the squirrels from the family room window, he feared the birds might soon have some competition.

Thankfully, the trio of squirrels appeared completely uninterested in the birdhouse as they scampered up and down the tree. But in a flash, the lead squirrel banked right, heading straight toward the full tray-style feeder.

Oh no. Darrell watched in frustrated amusement as the first squirrel scurried up the trunk and then flung himself onto the feeder. The squirrel swayed back and forth, looking as if he were on the Swinging Pirate Ship ride at the state fair, until he finally steadied himself on the feeder tray and began stuffing his cheeks full of bounty.

As the feeder swung close to the trunk, the squirrel jumped off and another squirrel jumped on. This was starting to look like Cirque du Soleil. Darrell shook his head. *Leave some for the birds!*

Darrell kept an eye on the trio of acrobatic seed thieves while he attached the outer side panels of the bookcase to the top and bottom panels. When he picked up the back panel and tried to attach it to the side panels, it didn't line up with the corresponding holes.

As he adjusted the base, there was a flurry of activity in the backyard. One squirrel swung from the feeder, stuffing his cheeks with seeds, as another dashed up the trunk, clearly wanting another turn on the swinging squirrel feeder.

As the confident little rodent's head mimicked the movement of the feeder, he made his jump—and missed his mark by inches. The over-confident squirrel face-planted in the leaves on the ground.

Darrell laughed so hard he thought the squirrel might hear him through the window. The stunned squirrel gave a little twitch of his head. Dejected and confused, the little thing dashed off into the woods behind their house.

"Got a little too cocky there, huh, buddy?" Darrell chuckled, turning back to the bookcase.

The back panel hung askew and there was a pile of extra screws.

Darrell shook his head in self-deprecating amusement.

"Guess I better give those instructions a once-over. I sure don't want to face-plant on this one."

Later that evening Darrell was thrilled to show his wife her brand-new, perfectly symmetrical bookcase.

PAWS & PONDER...

Have you ever experienced a face-plant moment? Looking back, what role did pride play in that experience? If you had been humble instead of arrogant, do you think it would have resulted in a different outcome? Why is humility a key component of godly wisdom?

Paws & Pray

Lord, I struggle with bouts of pride. I know you teach your followers to be humble, but I find myself wanting my own way and start to think of myself more highly than others, including you. Father, forgive me for listening to pride's whispers. Create in me a clean and humble heart.

23

A DIFFERENT PLAN

You can make many plans, but the LORD's purpose will prevail.

PROVERBS 19:21

LIKE MOST NEWLY MARRIED couples, Paul and Julie had many plans. From career aspirations to personal dreams, they had many goals and looked forward to achieving each one.

At first their plans fell right into place.

With two thriving careers and a beautiful new home, the young couple was overjoyed to discover they were pregnant. However, twelve weeks later, their dream was shattered by a heartbreaking miscarriage.

As Julie and Paul grieved and resolved to try again to have a baby, they decided it was the right time to bring a dog into their home.

A big supporter of rescuing animals, Julie convinced Paul to begin the search at their local shelter. They began visiting the shelter each weekend but were unable to find the right match. One afternoon, feeling disappointed after leaving the shelter empty-handed yet again, they noticed a local Great Dane rescue group was having an adoption event at a nearby store. So they went.

One regal-looking dog captured their attention and hearts, and they decided to pursue adopting him right then and there. A week later, he became part of their family.

Shep's large size and inquisitive, playful presence filled their home just as his loyal personality and companionship filled their hearts during months of doctor's appointments, fertility tests, and expensive treatments.

He was always available when Julie and Paul broke down and cried during the years of infertility. And Shep was a steady source of comfort as they surrendered their plans and empty arms to God and accepted his plan that they might not give birth to children of their own. The Great Dane's strong presence helped them through an incredibly difficult season.

When the couple decided to begin exploring adoption, Shep watched them fill out endless stacks of forms.

And then came the miraculous phone call from an adoption agency.

A baby boy needed a home. Were Paul and Julie ready to become parents?

Years after first dreaming of becoming parents, Paul and Julie were overjoyed to bring their son Riley home.

And faithful Shep was there to greet them.

The Great Dane's loyalty and devotion quickly extended to the smallest member of the family. Shep was never far from Riley's side. The large dog lay by Riley's crib while the baby slept, sat next to the bathtub while the infant got a bath, and took full advantage of the food dropped from Riley's high chair as he learned to feed himself. As protective as Shep was of his boy, Riley was enamored with his dog. Riley loved interacting with Shep—crawling after him when he got too far away and giggling at his slobbery kisses. Seeing the bond between their young son and their older dog warmed Paul's and Julie's hearts.

But they could never have imagined how that bond would come into play one night.

The winter after Riley's first birthday, during a bitterly cold night, Shep began pawing at Riley's closed bedroom door. The pawing quickly turned into deep, forceful barking.

The normally docile and aging dog was intent on getting into the baby's room.

When Paul and Julie opened the door, they were horrified to find it filled with smoke from a malfunctioning space heater, undetected by a faulty smoke detector. Julie ran to Riley, who was sound asleep in his crib, and scooped him up while Paul dialed 911.

"Your dog sure saved the day," a firefighter commented minutes later when the first responders arrived.

Paul rubbed his giant dog's head. He couldn't agree more. Shep had proven himself to be quite the hero. A rescued hero that hadn't been part of their initial life plan but ended up rescuing the child they thought would never come.

God had ordained a different plan for Paul and Julie—one they wouldn't trade for the world.[1]

PAWS & PONDER...

What plans have you made that have not yet been realized? How are you coping with the waiting? Would you be willing to exchange your plans for God's different plans? Will you, even now, surrender your deepest longings and dreams to him? You can trust him.

Paws & Pray

Father, it can be so hard to let go of a plan or a dream. Give me the strength to surrender mine to you. God, you tell me in your Word that your plans for me are good and for my good. Help my trust in you to outweigh my fear. Give me courage to wait for your answer and direction.

[1] My thanks to Paul Batura for allowing me to share his story, which was featured January 2019 on Fox News at https://www.foxnews.com/opinion/we-thought-we-were-rescuing-a-great-dane-but-heres-the-incredible-thing-that-happened-next.

24

WISE SNOOPY

There is precious treasure and oil in the dwelling of
the wise, but a foolish man swallows it up.

PROVERBS 21:20, NASB

SNOOPY AND WOODSTOCK, two-year-old boxers, looked very much alike, yet acted very differently.

Snoopy, whose black muzzle distinguished him from his white-muzzled brother, was rarely without a stuffed toy in his mouth. He loved his toys and was surprisingly gentle with each one.

That was not true for Woodstock.

It seemed as though Woodstock's mission was to destroy every toy he was given. Within minutes of receiving a new plush toy, Woodstock would rip it open and begin frantically pulling out the insides. Soon, the floor would be covered in white fuzz.

Meanwhile Snoopy would gingerly carry his new toy around—being careful to avoid his brother, who was still eviscerating his.

What amused Adam and Lisa, the duo's owners, was how Woodstock—without fail—would finish gutting his toy and then run to Snoopy wanting his. Snoopy would give a warning growl to his brother and turn away, keeping his fully intact toy safe in his mouth.

Woodstock would often whine and yip for several minutes before returning to his shredded toy.

One evening after tearing apart a toy donut, and then unsuccessfully trying to convince Snoopy to share his, Woodstock picked up a scrap of his flat donut and lay beside Snoopy.

Lisa couldn't help but laugh at the scene in front of her. One dog held a donut stuffy in his mouth while also guarding two other stuffed toys under his belly, and the other lay in the middle of a pile of fuzz, holding the remnants of a toy in his teeth.

"Oh, Woody," Lisa teased. "When are you gonna learn?"

Woodstock raised an eyebrow as she began to clean up the mess. She had a feeling that look meant *never*!

PAWS & PONDER...

In what ways do you tend to "swallow up" your treasures? Is this Proverb only refer-ring to monetary treasures? What other kinds of treasure might apply? What are some practical ways you can guard yourself against insisting on instant gratifica-tion or using up the resources God gives you?

Paws & Pray

Lord, guide me to know how and when to use the resources you have given me. Give me strength to gather and save my treasures. Father, I want to save wisely, be more generous, and honor you with what you have entrusted to me.

A friend is always loyal, and a brother is born
to help in time of need.

PROVERBS 17:17

25

SHY AND SEQUOIA

Blessed is the one who finds wisdom, and the one who gets understanding.

PROVERBS 3:13, ESV

WHEN GAYLE ADOPTED one-year-old Shy—a pure-white Siberian husky with crystal blue eyes—she quickly discovered the dog was energy contained in white fur. Shy was rambunctious, playful, and always on the move, unless she was sleeping.

However, when Gayle found herself in the midst of a difficult season—a situation that caused her great emotional pain and distress—Shy became calm. Shy instantly sensed what Gayle needed. She would lie at Gayle's feet for hours, follow her from room to room, and sit with her as she cried. The once-hyperactive dog suddenly became her protective comforter. If Gayle was hurting, Shy was right beside her. She saw Gayle through a difficult time.

Then Gayle met Andy, and their mutual love of dogs became a starting point for conversations. They both had Siberian huskies! Andy loved hearing Gayle's stories about Shy, and she enjoyed Andy's tales about his dog, Sequoia. The dog lovers and their dogs became one family when Andy and Gayle eventually married.

One of Gayle's favorite Sequoia stories took place before she even knew Andy. His aunt Mary, a gentle woman with physical and mental challenges, was coming to visit for the weekend, and Andy was worried about how Sequoia would interact with her. Sequoia was a large dog with a deep, intimidating bark that made him sound vicious. Andy knew

Sequoia was actually a cuddly giant, but he was concerned that Sequoia would frighten his aunt. Andy tried to teach his canine buddy to tone it down, but nothing seemed to work.

Mary arrived at Andy's house, and he introduced her to Sequoia. Andy noticed she was tentative about touching him, and she kept a safe distance from the dog. Yet Mary's eyes never wandered far from Sequoia.

When Sequoia headed to the back door, Andy jumped up to intercept him before the husky could roar to be let out. But to Andy's amazement, his dog released the softest muffled woof he had ever heard him make. Andy glanced at Aunt Mary, who sat quietly watching Sequoia.

When the dog came back in, he calmly walked to Mary and sat down at her feet. Andy was overjoyed as he watched Mary stroke Sequoia's thick fur.

The entire weekend was eye-opening for Andy. Even though he had never trained Sequoia to be an assist dog, the husky intuitively sensed Mary's needs and would give a short, soft bark whenever she wanted to get up—alerting Andy to come help her. Wherever Mary went in Andy's house, Sequoia followed, always staying within an arm's reach of her.

Sequoia's protectiveness and gentleness inspired Andy and left a lasting impression on Aunt Mary. From that time on, whenever Andy called her, the first question she asked was always, "How's Sequoia?"

Shy and Sequoia—two large dogs who at first glance seemed loud and rambunctious, but whose actions, intuition, and understanding forever impacted the lives of those who were blessed to know them, especially Gayle and Andy.

PAWS & PONDER...

Has your life been impacted by another person's wisdom and understanding? What kind of blessings did you receive from interacting with that person? Is there a situation you are facing that requires wisdom and understanding? Take a few minutes to ask God, the giver of wisdom, to help you.

Paws & Pray

Father God, thank you for allowing me to live on a planet full of animals, whose unconditional love and understanding point me to you. Lord, I want to be a wise and understanding person. Draw me to your Word and teach me how to bless others.

2 6

ӨH, CAPONE!

The wise store up knowledge, but the mouth of a fool invites ruin.

PROVERBS 10:14, NIV

"**OH, CAPONE!**" is a phrase often heard in Babette's house.

With an appetite inversely proportional to his size, her eighteen-pound Miniature Pinscher has spent most of his days looking for food. He has tried to ingest anything he could get his mouth around—whether it was edible or not.

It started when Babette discovered her little chowhound trash-diving one evening. Babette began keeping the trash can in a cupboard—secured with a rubber band to the knob of the adjoining cupboard so Capone couldn't open it.

One night, after throwing out a rotisserie chicken carcass, a bolt of lightning lit up the sky, followed by a deafening clap of thunder that shook the house. Babette and her husband heard a loud cracking sound and then a huge crash.

"A tree's down!" They ran out the door to check on their neighbors. An eighty-foot oak had been hit by lightning and a gigantic branch had landed on the neighbors' house. No one was hurt, but there was damage to the chimney and roof.

A half hour later, Babette returned to a mess inside the house. The cupboard door was open and the trash can had been pulled out and was lying on its side. There was no sign of the chicken carcass in the trash strewn across the floor. In the corner of the kitchen was Capone with guilt written all over his face and a belly so swollen it appeared as though he was carrying a litter of twelve puppies!

"Oh, Capone," Babette lamented. "What have you done?"

She rushed him to the emergency vet, where X-rays confirmed that Capone had indeed ingested the entire chicken's skeletal remains. Somehow, he had gobbled everything whole. It was still intact inside of his distended stomach! Babette stayed with Capone for hours in the exam room as the vet gave him medicine to try to expel the chicken.

The medicine eventually worked, and four X-rays later (at one hundred dollars per image) the vet finally declared Capone carcass free. The entire ordeal cost twelve hundred dollars and left Capone with a permanent description in his file: Capone—the chicken carcass dog.

Babette hoped the chicken caper would teach Capone a lesson.

Months went by with no incidents. As summer was winding down, Babette and her husband decided to apply fresh caulk around the panes of their century-old farmhouse windows. Capone seemed interested in what they were doing, but their focus was on the windows, not him. Finally, the job was done, and it was time to clean up and take showers. About an hour later they walked downstairs and there was Capone—with white putty on his whiskers. The Min Pin had licked the caulk from each and every pane he could reach.

"Oh, Capone . . ." Babette gasped, frantic to find the tube of caulk.

When she found it, she didn't see any poison warning, but her instincts said, *Call the vet.*

After explaining the situation to the receptionist, Babette cringed when the woman said, "Oh, I remember Capone. He's the chicken carcass dog, right?"

"Yes," Babette said. "That's him."

The vet had never treated a dog that had eaten caulk before, but he decided the best course of action would be to induce vomiting with doses of hydrogen peroxide. Thankfully, it worked.

As it did months later when Capone raided the kids' Easter baskets and scarfed down all the Hershey kisses. And again when he ate a bar of Dial soap.

Oh, Capone . . .

PAWS & PONDER...

You probably don't ever plan to eat a whole chicken carcass (bones and all) or a tube of caulk, and yet "ruin" could still be invited in and out of your mouth. How often have you eaten something you knew wasn't healthy for you? Or said something unkind without even thinking? In what ways can wisdom protect you from such ruin? And how do you store that knowledge?

Paws & Pray

God, you are the Author and Creator of wisdom. I often do and say things without even thinking of the consequences for myself or for others. Draw my heart and mind to you that I might speak with integrity and grace. Put your love in my heart and your words in my mouth.

27

SIMPLE KINDNESS

If you want to be happy, be kind to the poor;

it is a sin to despise anyone.

PROVERBS 14:21, GNT

TINA LOOKED AT THE STACK of bills on the counter. She didn't need to log in to her bank account to know that she wouldn't be able to pay them all this month. Her shoulders slumped as she pulled last night's tuna casserole from the refrigerator. She dished out a serving to reheat in the microwave.

Tina had been working for the past six months as an administrative assistant at a tire store—a big improvement from the late shift she had been working at the pizza place. But money was still tight.

Will I ever get ahead?

When the microwave timer went off, Tina took her plate outside on the deck. Her townhouse backed up to a nature reserve, giving her a glorious view from her backyard.

As she took her first bite, she heard a rustling sound in the bushes. Assuming the noise to be squirrels at play, she continued to eat. But when the rustling turned into a pitiful meow, Tina set her plate aside and stood up to get a better look. A gray and white cat emerged from a nandina bush.

"Well, hello," Tina said to the unexpected visitor. "I've never seen you around here before."

She expected the cat to run away, but it didn't even look up. It kept walking toward Tina's deck—its little nose pressed to the ground.

"You're a confident little cat, aren't you?"

The cat continued walking, lifting its nose every few steps to sniff the air before making it to the stairs of Tina's deck. It cautiously climbed up.

Tina knelt in front of the haggard-looking cat, whose matted fur and noticeable ribs tugged at Tina's heart. She stretched her hand toward the little animal who again raised its nose as if catching a new scent. Now just a foot away, Tina noticed the cat's unfocused, glassy eyes. She snapped her fingers, but the cat did not react at all. Tina surmised the stray could neither see nor hear.

"Oh, kitty," she said. "What happened to you?"

The cat rubbed against Tina's leg, then lifted her nose into the air again—something smelled good.

The tuna casserole.

Without a second thought, Tina put her plate in front of the cat who devoured it in less than ten minutes. After eating her fill, the cat licked her front paws, and then lay down on Tina's outdoor rug.

Tina sat with the cat until the sun dropped below the horizon. Before turning in for the night, she set out a bowl of milk and spread a thick blanket beside the cat.

"Goodnight, little kitty."

The next morning the cat was gone.

Tina hoped she would see the cat again, but she never did. The little cat was a fighter and had clearly found a way to keep going, no matter what life threw at her—a way that clearly included the kindness of strangers.

Three weeks later, Tina opened her mailbox to find a card from an aunt she hadn't seen in ten years. The aunt wrote that she felt led to send Tina a little gift, and she had enclosed a check.

Tina's eyes blurred with tears at this unexpected gift, and she immediately thought of the feline visitor. Maybe Tina's simple act of kindness was being repaid.

PAWS & PONDER . . .

In what ways does being kind to the poor make us happy? Do you think this proverb applies only to those who are poor financially? To whom else might this verse apply? What are some practical ways you could show kindness to the poor?

Paws & Pray

God, thank you for caring about me and meeting my needs, often by stirring the hearts of others to help. Would you stir my heart to show kindness to the poor—the poor in spirit as well as those struggling financially. Fill my heart to overflowing with love for you so that I can gladly share your lovingkindness with those in need.

28

A HARDY DOG

The discerning heart seeks knowledge, but
the mouth of a fool feeds on folly.

PROVERBS 15:14, NIV

"HAVE YOU SEEN THE BEAGLE hanging out near the barn?" Crystal Sides's husband, Tracy, asked her one morning as he opened the back door.

"No," she said emphatically, then added, "we are *not* getting another animal."

Living on a farm instead of in the city was a dream come true for Crystal. She had always loved animals and open spaces. But life on a farm also meant the constant care of their animal menagerie—chickens, cats, dogs, and a donkey—and the always dreaded vet bills.

A few days later, Crystal was in the kitchen when her daughter Hope ran into the house. "Mom, have you seen the dog down by the barn? She is so sweet."

Hope's eyes shone with excitement.

"We are not getting another animal," Crystal repeated the response she had given Tracy. "I'm sure she belongs to someone and will find her way home soon."

Hope couldn't hide her disappointment as she ran out the door.

"We cannot get another animal," Crystal announced to the empty kitchen.

Several weeks passed without any more mention of the mysterious beagle. Then one Sunday morning as the family was leaving for church, Hope shouted, "There she is! Look, Mom."

Tucked close to the side of their barn was a lemon-yellow beagle that looked starved and terrified. She had no collar and was covered with flea bites.

Hope quietly got out of the car and called to the emaciated dog. Unbeknownst to Crystal, Hope had been leaving a little food for her each night, and over time she had begun to earn the animal's trust.

The pitiful little beagle took a few timid steps toward Hope. With each step, she looked up at Hope, staring at the face of her rescuer. Yet when Crystal and Tracy slowly approached, the dog ran away.

"Mom—"

"Yes," Crystal answered her daughter before she could finish her question, "if we can't find her owner or if she isn't safe where she came from, we can keep her." More and more, Crystal was suspecting the latter. It wasn't long before the beagle officially became part of the family.

They named her Hardy—a fitting name for a dog who had endured so much on her journey to find a new and caring family.

Crystal, Tracy, and Hope spent a lot of time with Hardy, working to gain her trust and care for her needs. It was obvious she had suffered abuse in the past. She didn't want to be touched at first, which is typical of animals who've been hurt by human hands. But with patience, gentleness, and compassion, Hardy eventually learned she was safe.

And yet even after learning that Crystal, Tracy, and Hope could be trusted, Hardy still greeted them with a pointed stare that pierced their souls. *Is it really safe to come to you?*

A year later, Crystal was at the vet clinic with Hardy. During an examination, the doctor discovered extensive heartworm damage in Hardy's heart and lungs. The care would be costly, but Crystal didn't mind paying those bills or taking care of Hardy as her health began to significantly decline. In fact, Hardy's new family made it their mission to give her the best life possible while she was still with them.

Hardy might not have known safety or gentleness in her early years, but because she was cautiously willing to trust again, she experienced the life-changing power of kindness and love at the end of her life.

PAWS & PONDER . . .

Hardy found it very difficult to trust humans, even those who wanted to help her. Can you relate to Hardy's reluctance to trust others? Why is discernment a necessary part of trust? Would you be willing to trust God in one small area today and allow him to prove that he is trustworthy?

Paws & Pray

Lord, you are trustworthy, and yet I often find it difficult to fully trust you. Would you reveal your character to me in your Word and help me embrace your truth more? Help me discern evidence of your love for me and find ways to demonstrate that love and kindness to others.

29

A FIERCE LOVE

Don't turn your back on wisdom, for she will protect you.

Love her, and she will guard you.

PROVERBS 4:6

VICKY BELIEVED SHE HAD hit the proverbial jackpot when she adopted nine-week-old Misty from the SPCA. Even at such a young age, it seemed as if the shepherd mix was grateful to have been given a home that she was determined to be the best-behaved dog around. And she was.

Misty never had an accident inside the house, never chewed anything other than her own toys, and barked only when she needed to go out or to alert Vicky that someone was at the door. Misty truly seemed like the ideal dog. Some of Vicky's friends were mildly annoyed that their dogs did not have such pristine reputations.

Misty's ideal status only increased after Vicky and her husband, Rick, welcomed two sons into their family a year apart. Misty didn't seem to mind sharing Vicky and Rick's attention. Instead, she delighted in the presence of two more humans to love. She often slept in the same room with the boys, lay beside them on the floor when they played, and sat in the kitchen with them while they ate.

Misty was a fierce and loyal companion—something Vicky was grateful for the day a man knocked on the door.

After securing her two-year-old in his high chair, Vicky answered the door with her one-year-old in her arms. Misty followed Vicky to the door, then sat off to the side, just out of the man's view.

The man said he was selling cleaning products and wanted to give Vicky a demonstration. Vicky pointed to the child in her arms and laughed. "I'm sorry. I have my hands full at the moment. Thanks, but I'm not interested."

The man persisted, however, continuing to talk about the product and urging her to give him a few minutes of her time. Vicky became annoyed and went to close the door, but the man grabbed the door and attempted to jerk it open. As he did, Misty charged from her position, leapt past Vicky, and released a menacing growl. Vicky had never heard such a sound come from her dog. Misty chased the man down the sidewalk, the cleaning supplies dropping from his hands as he took off running. Vicky allowed Misty to get several houses away before she called her to come back. Vicky saw no trace of the man after that, and he never returned for his cleaning supplies.

Vicky has no idea what might have happened that day, but thanks to Misty she doesn't need to worry about it. Misty was there to protect her family—a family she fiercely loved. And a family who fiercely loved her right back.

PAWS & PONDER...

How does wisdom protect you? How does wisdom guard you? What does it mean to protect and love wisdom? What are practical ways you can do that? How has wisdom protected you in the past? 🐾

_____   _____

Paws & Pray

God, thank you for the gift of wisdom. Help me never to turn my back on your gift but cherish and protect it. Allow wisdom to guard my life so that others will see you in me.

The horse is made ready for the day of battle,

but the victory belongs to the LORD.

PROVERBS 21:31, ESV

30

ʜUMBLE ʙEGINNINGS

Pride brings a person low, but the lowly in spirit gain honor.

PROVERBS 29:23, NIV

TO TEN-YEAR-OLD CAITLYN, the eight hundred dollars her father spent on their newest pony seemed like a fortune. And yet she had heard her father say that he got a great deal on the pony named Honey because the six-year-old mare couldn't cut it as a trail horse. He described her as a failed trail pony.

The description seemed harsh to Caitlyn. Maybe Honey just didn't like carrying strangers on her back every day over the same old trails.

She sure wouldn't like that. Caitlyn much preferred the show ring where she got to do jumps and routines with her horses.

Normally shy and guarded, Caitlyn felt like a different person in the show ring. There, she was in control. Leading a thousand-pound animal around a ring and telling it with her body cues where to go and what to do made her feel powerful and confident. And for a girl with little control over where she went and what she did each day, it was a glorious feeling.

It made her feel alive and . . . happy.

As Honey settled into her paddock, Caitlyn began spending more and more time with her. The mare was the first American Paint pony the family had ever owned, and Caitlyn was captivated by her coloring—a honey-colored body, white legs, and a white head with brilliant blue eyes that were surrounded with what looked like black eyeliner.

Caitlyn thought she was the most beautiful pony in the world. "You really do look like honey," she told the pony.

Honey quickly became Caitlyn's best friend and confidant—the keeper of her secrets, the listener of her dreams.

She also became her favorite riding partner.

Sensing Honey's intelligence and hunger to learn, Caitlyn asked her father if she could start training Honey as a hunter/jumper. The two of them would learn to navigate through a series of jumps of varying heights and widths.

Her father agreed, and Honey began her training.

Although the pony had failed at trail riding, she excelled at jumping and truly seemed to love it.

Caitlyn saw in Honey's eyes the same passion for the ring that she felt herself.

Within months Caitlyn was astride Honey, leading her through her first junior hunter/jumper competition.

Honey won.

Her father was thrilled with the prestigious ribbon, but Caitlyn was thrilled to see Honey happy.

"I knew you weren't a failure," she whispered in Honey's ear as she brushed the pony's coat after the show. "You are a champion!"

Over the years Honey won numerous competitions.

Caitlyn was happy with what she and Honey accomplished, but what made her even happier was being with her pony and doing what they loved together.

A girl and her pony, who saw in each other something far more valuable than ribbons or money or fame—the gift of friendship.

PAWS & PONDER...

In what ways can pride "bring a person low"? Have you ever seen this happen in someone's life? Have you ever been brought low because of your pride? Conversely, have you ever witnessed a truly humble person gain honor? In what ways might someone gain honor as a result of their humility?

Paws & Pray

Jesus, thank you for demonstrating the ultimate act of humility by leaving your rightful place in heaven to come to earth and die for my sin. That is a priceless gift to me. Lord, help me to accept your sacrificial gift so that I can have a relationship with you. Teach me to be humble and loving and value you as my most trusted friend.

31

THE GUILT WALK

Whoever walks in integrity walks securely, but whoever
takes crooked paths will be found out.

PROVERBS 10:9, NIV

"MOLLIE, WHAT HAVE YOU BEEN UP TO?"
Christine always knew when Mollie, her three-year-old hound mix, had completed a successful mission to confiscate a forbidden item from somewhere in their house. Instead of bounding into a room like she normally did, Mollie would gingerly hug the perimeter of the room, carrying the stolen goods in her mouth. She would slowly weave around side tables, step over electrical cords, and squeeze behind chairs. Her family called it the "guilt walk"—a purposeful walk with her head down to avoid eye contact with her humans.

The behavior amused her family as much as it frustrated them.

"Mom, Mollie stole my teddy bear!"

"Mom, Mollie chewed a hole in my shoe!"

"Mom, Mollie grabbed my pencil!"

Not a week went by without at least one family member broadcasting throughout the house that another Mollie grab-and-go had gone down.

Christine decided to hire a dog trainer to "cure" Mollie of her kleptomania. Even though the trainer came several times over the course of two months, the lanky dog couldn't resist the allure of forbidden items.

Mollie easily could have run into another room with her contraband, leaving her humans none the wiser. But Mollie always insisted on slinking in plain sight around the room where her family gathered. She operated on the "I can't see you, so you can't see me" theory of criminal activity. Unfortunately, her thievery was detected every time—maybe not on the first lap around the obstacle-like course, but on subsequent ones.

Christine and her family have resigned themselves to Mollie's pilfering ways and love her despite the quirky behavior. After all, when something goes missing, they know who to track down first.

"Mom! My new socks are missing!"

PAWS & PONDER . . .

Does Mollie's "guilt walk" remind you of how you react when you sin? What crooked paths do you need to be on guard against taking? *Merriam-Webster* defines integrity as "firm adherence to a code of especially moral or artistic values." How does walking in integrity give a person security? How might you walk purposefully in integrity today?

Paws & Pray

Lord, I need help every day to follow you. I am so easily pulled onto the crooked path by my own desires, greed, and pride. I confess my sin to you and ask that you set my feet on your straight path—the path of integrity and life.

3 2

ℒITTLE ℬELLA

The generous will prosper; those who refresh
others will themselves be refreshed.

PROVERBS 11:25

"MOM, NO ONE WANTS HER because of her cherry eye. The poor thing needs a home, and you need a friend. Won't you at least consider it?"

Ronda listened as her son Levi presented his case to make the chihuahua puppy part of their family.

Yes, I do need a friend. But a puppy with an eye condition? Ronda had never even heard of a "cherry eye" before, but a quick Google search gave her the answer: A condition that causes a gland in a dog's eye to protrude, appearing as a red mass outside of the eye.

Ronda had grown up with dogs, but they were always big and kept outside. Her ex-husband had never wanted a dog. But of course, now things were different. She was in her midforties, recovering from breast cancer, grieving the end of her marriage—something she had fought hard to avoid—and facing an empty house as her sons Levi and Ethan returned to college and work.

As she looked at Levi's concerned face, her heart began to soften. *Maybe having a little companion wouldn't be such a bad idea.* Besides, she knew more than most how wretched it is to feel unwanted or unchosen, and no one, not even a dog, should ever have to feel that way. So she agreed to meet the puppy the next day.

Of course, her son interpreted "meet the puppy" as an invitation to bring the two-pounder to the hospital where Ronda worked. Everyone instantly fell in love with the tiny dog. Levi made it impossible for his mom to say anything other than yes! Ronda named her Bella and welcomed her into her life that same evening.

In the morning, Ronda made an appointment with the vet to examine Bella. The vet recommended surgery.

"Will it affect her sight?" Ronda asked. The doctor assured her that the surgery was routine. If left untreated, the protruding gland could become infected or eventually cause dry eye.

Everything went well. Bella was a trouper, and with Ronda's attentive care, she recovered quickly and soon settled into her new home. Ronda bonded with the tiny dog in a way she never thought possible. Bella quickly became more than her dog; she became her constant companion. Ronda loved carrying Bella everywhere in the pink dog-carrier bag she had bought—to the store, to visit Ronda's coworkers at the hospital, and on family vacations.

Of course, Bella couldn't always join Ronda on an outing, but when the two were reunited after a long day of work or errands, little Bella let her excitement out with wiggles, jumps, and rollovers for belly rubs. Bella's love filled the house. Ronda's tears never fell unnoticed because Bella was there to comfort her. And when Ronda learned she had stage four liver cancer, Bella was there to steady her.

The tiny dog remained by Ronda's side as she endured a year of outpatient chemotherapy. And Bella waited at home with Ronda's cousin while Ronda had surgery.

It was a long, painful, and exhausting journey, but a year after Ronda started treatment, she received news that her cancer was gone.

"Bella, this is definitely worth celebrating," Ronda said, wiping away grateful tears. Bella responded with lots of kisses and enjoyed a cup of doggie ice cream.

The first time Ronda saw Bella, she thought she was rescuing a little dog no one wanted. Now Ronda knows that Bella was really the one who rescued her.

PAWS & PONDER...

Ronda thought she was rescuing Bella, but little did she know her dog would, in many ways, rescue her simply by being there. Who has been there for you during a hard season? Who is someone who might need you to be there—to simply sit and listen and be present?

_____ _____

Paws & Pray

Lord, so many people are hurting today, facing incredibly difficult circumstances. Let each one of them be aware of your presence today. Shine the light of your love and hope where there is darkness and despair and whisper your truth over each one. And Lord, equip and enable me to see the needs of people in my life and be willing to simply be there for them. When I need help, give me courage to reach out to others, too.

3 3

A LONGING FULFILLED

The hopes of the godly result in happiness, but the

expectations of the wicked come to nothing.

PROVERBS 10:28

"MOM! There's a cat in our ditch!" twelve-year-old Andrew exclaimed, bursting through the back door. "It's not a fox; it's a cat!"

Ella, eight, jumped up. Her homework sheet went flying as she ran to her brother.

"What?" she shrieked. "Are you serious?"

"Come on," Andrew urged. "You too, Mom, come on!"

Jen pushed the cutting board filled with chopped vegetables to the center of the kitchen island—safe from the reach of their counter-surfing Golden retriever, Bailey. She couldn't help but smile at her animated children. They were talking so fast she could barely understand what they were saying. She heard *ditch, bushy-tailed, not fox, cat!*

"We need to get her food," Andrew declared.

"It's a *girl* cat?" Ella shrieked again, clapping her hands.

Andrew nodded. "I think so; it's all fluffy."

Jen thought her daughter was going to swoon.

"A fluffy cat of my very own," Ella whispered.

"Okay, you two," Jen said, trying to temper the escalating euphoria. "The cat probably belongs to someone."

Ella's intense look got Jen's attention. "Mommy," Ella said as if she were talking to a child, "this is the cat we have prayed for. I just know it."

After the children had begged Jen and her husband for a cat for years,

Jen finally told her kids that if they ever found a stray cat, they could feed it and take care of it—outside. Jen had a severe allergy to cats that made keeping a cat in the house impossible.

But that didn't deter her determined kids. When Andrew was seven, he began praying every night for a cat. Soon his three-year-old sister joined him for the nightly petition. After several months passed without a cat falling from heaven like manna, the siblings' prayers began to dwindle to once every couple of weeks. When several years passed without a stray cat appearing on their doorstep, the prayers had all but stopped.

But now, taking charge with complete confidence, Ella opened the refrigerator, took a slice of deli turkey, and announced, "My cat likes turkey."

I guess Ella knows, Jen thought, following her kids outside.

Sure enough, there in the drainage ditch was a cat. The poor thing looked pitifully thin, with leaves and pine needles sticking to her coat and matted fur along her chest. When the three of them approached, she retreated into the large pipe that ran under the driveway. Andrew took the piece of turkey from Ella and squatted in the ditch. He didn't move a muscle.

Within minutes the nervous cat approached. She took a tentative nibble, then devoured the entire slice. Ella ran in the house to get more. Jen watched as the cat climbed into her son's lap. His face beamed with joy.

Ella returned with the entire package of Boar's Head turkey. Jen started to protest, but she took one look at the poor cat and decided the least the animal deserved was $10.99-a-pound lunch meat.

Over the next few weeks, Jen sent messages to the neighborhood email group asking if anyone had lost a cat. The family even put up a few signs. But no one ever claimed Foxy, Ella's choice for the stray's name.

A month later, the family was sitting on the back deck finishing dinner when Foxy jumped up on the table. Bailey sprang from her nap to greet the cat with a sniff. Jen still couldn't believe the friendship the two had formed. Ella petted the much healthier cat as she silently walked past Ella's plate. Foxy then leapt from the table onto Andrew's lap and began purring.

"See, Mommy," Ella said with a smile. "God sent us a cat. It just took him a while to find us the right one."

PAWS & PONDER...

Waiting on the Lord is a common theme throughout the Bible. Psalm 27:14 says that a person should be brave and courageous as he or she waits on the Lord. Why do you think waiting on God requires bravery and courage? What are you waiting for God to do? Have you grown weary in the waiting? Will you recommit to wait for his leading on a specific request today—trusting his timing and will?

Paws & Pray

God, waiting can be so hard. Would you grant me strength and courage to wait? Help me to trust your timing of the plans you have for me. As I wait on you, help me to encourage others as they wait.

34

PUGSLEY

A sluggard buries his hand in the dish; he will

not even bring it back to his mouth!

PROVERBS 19:24, NIV

SUSAN HAD NEVER SEEN HER DOG, Pugsley, look more pitiful than when she picked him up from the veterinary hospital after
his dental cleaning. The seven-year-old pug trembled as the technician
handed him to Susan.

"He did great," the tech said, "but I know he's ready to get out of
here."

Susan offered an apologetic smile. "I don't know why he's so frightened to come here. You guys are great. He's just a big ol' scaredy-cat,
aren't ya, boy?"

After a few parting instructions from the tech, Susan took Pugsley
home, where he promptly fell asleep. After listening to him snore for
several hours, Susan got up to prepare his dinner. The vet tech had suggested softening his kibble or giving him canned food for the next few
days, in case his mouth was a little sore from the procedure. So Susan
popped open a can of food and scooped it into Pugsley's ceramic bowl.

"Come, Pugsley, it's din-din time," she called.

The pug opened an eye but did not move a muscle.

"Pugsley," she tried again. "Come eat your dinner."

Pugsley got up, turned in a circle, then once again curled up in a
ball on the sofa.

Susan carried the bowl of food to Pugsley and held it under his nose.

He looked from his bowl to Susan, then back to his bowl. Finally, he lowered his head over his bowl and began to eat.

Susan felt guilty for letting her dog eat while lying on the furniture. *Just this once—because he's been through such an ordeal,* she assured herself.

The next day, when Pugsley again refused to come into the kitchen to eat, Susan tried to stand strong.

"Pugsley, you have to come *in here* to eat. Come here," she commanded.

Her dog stepped one paw into the kitchen and then lay down. Two big round eyes stared beseechingly at her.

"Oh, all right," Susan sighed. "At least you're in the kitchen."

She again brought his bowl to him, where he leisurely ate with his front half on the kitchen's tile floor and his back half on the family room carpet.

After four days of catering to her dog—including hand-feeding him—Susan realized her dog had become quite lazy and spoiled. At his last feeding, he didn't even lower his head to the bowl, but simply waited for Susan to bring the kibble to his mouth. She knew she needed to bring Pugsley back to reality. So the following day she poured a scoop of kibble into his food bowl and placed it next to his water bowl on the floor.

"Pugsley," she called out. "Dinner!"

Pugsley sashayed into the kitchen where he sat with his hind end on the carpet and his front paws on the tile.

"Oh no, you don't," Susan chided. "You are coming in here to eat today, mister."

Pugsley turned the full force of his sad puppy eyes on her, but Susan was resolved.

The standoff lasted several hours, during which time Susan completed a lengthy list of household chores, while Pugsley stared longingly at the food bowl lying ten feet away from him.

Finally, after his pleading looks and incessant whining went unanswered, the disgruntled pug sulked his way into the kitchen, lowered his head over his bowl, and surrendered to his hunger.

Twenty minutes later Susan laughed out loud as Pugsley sank to the floor with his head on his food bowl and fell sound asleep.

Susan shook her head, as she carried the pug to his bed. "You silly dog. You may be a scaredy-cat and a lazybones, but I sure do love you."

PAWS & PONDER . . .

A one-time indulgence resulted in an unintended pattern for Susan and Pugsley. Have you ever experienced a similar result? How did you break the pattern? Or maybe you are still stuck in that pattern. If so, what steps can you take today to break free of the destructive pattern of laziness and/or overindulgence?

Paws & Pray

Lord, I love to be comfortable and content, but sometimes those things can become bad habits if I'm not careful. I sometimes opt to be lazy and self-indulgent when I should be doing the work you've given me to do. Help me to fight against those destructive patterns so I can live a full and purposeful life.

Do not withhold good from those who deserve it
when it's in your power to help them.

PROVERBS 3:27

35

ℒET'S ℊO, ℬULLET

The fear of man lays a snare, but whoever trusts in the Lord is safe.

PROVERBS 29:25, ESV

ICE PELLETS STUNG SARAH'S FACE as she walked her year-old dog, Bullet, early one February morning. No one else was out yet. As the sleet increased, Sarah pulled her hat over her ears and picked up speed, doing her best to avoid icy spots on the sidewalk.

"Only for you, Bullet. Only for you would I walk in the freezing cold before dawn." Bullet gave her a quick glance, but he knew exactly where they were headed and didn't want to waste time getting there.

With her husband, Kory, away on business, and her workday full of back-to-back meetings, Sarah knew Bullet needed to burn off some energy at the dog park before being left at home for the day.

When they arrived, they had the park to themselves. Sarah closed the gate behind her and unsnapped the leash from Bullet's collar. "Go on. Have fun," she said, watching him run around the inside perimeter of the enclosure. *You've made so much progress since we met you at the animal shelter, Bullet.*

Six months earlier, the Lab mix had bonded readily to Sarah, seeking her out, staying close by, gladly accepting pets and belly rubs, but he was much more nervous around men. At times he would even cower or tremble in their presence.

Trying to better understand the reason behind her dog's fear and how she might better help him, Sarah had reached out to the animal shelter for more information. It had broken her heart to discover the horrific abuse her dog had suffered at the hands of his previous owner—a man with no patience for an exuberant puppy.

Sarah and Kory had worked hard to gain Bullet's trust. And while it had taken several months, Bullet was finally starting to let Kory give him a belly rub or hand him a treat. But Kory was the only man Bullet would approach. He still wouldn't come near Sarah's dad, who loved dogs and visited often.

"It's a work in progress," her dad would say, shrugging off Bullet's behavior. "I'll win him over one of these days."

This morning Bullet came bounding to Sarah—clearly wanting to play. She glanced around in hopes of finding a forgotten ball she could throw. *Yes!* There was a tennis ball near the picnic tables, so she quickly made her way to the covered shelter. Bullet began jumping with anticipation, as Sarah placed the ball on the ground.

"Do you want it? You'd better start running," Sarah said playfully.

She swung her leg out to kick the ball and . . . slipped on a patch of black ice that had been hidden under the snow. Her feet flew out from under her as she fell over backward, instinctively putting her hands behind her to break her fall.

As she tried to get up, everything seemed to be spinning, and intense pain was shooting up and down her arms.

Something is wrong with my wrists. I can't make it home with Bullet. I can't hold his leash. I need to get help. She gritted her teeth against the pain as she inched one hand slowly to her pocket and pulled out her phone. She could barely dial her parents' number.

Her dad said he was on his way.

Sarah made her way to the picnic tables a few yards away. It seemed like miles. When she got to a table, she was so exhausted and dizzy she could barely call Bullet's name. The reality of the situation made the pain worse.

How would she get Bullet to go to her dad and into his car?

Bullet sat several feet away from Sarah, head tilted, eyes fixed on her. Then he resumed his exploration of the park but kept a watchful eye on her.

While she waited for her dad, Sarah tried to think how this was going to play out. And then her dad was there. He drove his SUV straight down the hill path and up to the dog park gate. When he got out of the car, Sarah watched helplessly. What would Bullet do? They were enclosed inside the fenced park, but Bullet would still be nearly impossible to catch if he avoided her dad as he had always done before.

Bullet looked at Sarah, and without her speaking a word, he seemed to sense that something was wrong. He began walking toward her dad. He stopped a few feet away and lowered his head as Sarah's dad slowly moved toward him with the leash he'd brought. Bullet stayed still and allowed him to clip the leash to his collar.

"Let's go, Bullet," he said. Immediately Bullet jumped in the back seat of the car.

Sarah couldn't believe what had just happened.

"Told you he would come around," her dad said with a wink, as he came back and helped Sarah to the car.

And indeed Bullet did. After getting medical treatment for two broken wrists, Sarah and her husband decided it would be best if she and Bullet stayed with her parents for six weeks while she healed. Bullet's fear of Sarah's dad healed, too, as they bonded with each other, eventually becoming the very best of friends.

PAWS & PONDER...

While Bullet's fear of men was understandable and justified—why could that fear have been a "snare" for him in this situation? What might have happened if Bullet hadn't trusted Sarah's father? What is the difference between being cautious and being fearful? Is it easy for you to shrug off what others think of you or what they can do to you? How does trusting in the Lord keep you safe?

Paws & Pray

Father God, help me to trust in you more and more each day. Sometimes it is difficult for me to remember that you are bigger and greater and stronger than my fears. Open my eyes to see the truth—that no one can harm my soul or take me away from you. Lord, the world tells me I have much to fear, but you tell me not to be afraid. Today, I claim that. Bolster my courage!

36

SUGAR'S OFFERING

Honor the LORD with your wealth and with the best part of

everything you produce. Then he will fill your barns with grain,

and your vats will overflow with good wine.

PROVERBS 3:9-10

SOPHIE PATTED THE MESH lounge chair on the deck, inviting her cat, Sugar, to join her. The gray and black American shorthair leapt onto the chair, covering up Sophie's math book as she made herself comfortable. The fifteen-year-old laughed.

"I feel the same way about math," Sophie said, giggling as she gave the cat a thorough scratch behind her ears.

Sugar purred approvingly.

"Sophie!" her dad called from inside the house. "Your killing-machine cat has left you another offering of devotion at the front door."

"Ugh, not again!" the teenager moaned. "I know I rescued you, Sugar, but you really don't need to bring me disgusting gifts."

Sophie grabbed a bag and headed to Sugar's latest victim—a tail-less squirrel. *Ew! This is the second one this month.* She tried not to breathe too deeply as she scooped up the poor creature.

She loved everything about Sugar—her first pet—except this!

None of her friends with cats had ever mentioned this disturbing behavior. But then again, they all had cats that had been raised indoors. Maybe this only happened with cats who had lived outdoors before being rescued.

As Sophie closed the lid of the trash can, a van pulled into the drive-way. *The washing machine repairman. Mom will definitely be happy to see him!* Sophie thought as she returned to her homework. The appliance had been on the fritz for days, and laundry was piling up.

Sugar was still sprawled on the math book; she didn't appear to have moved an inch since Sophie left.

The two worked in companionable silence for nearly twenty minutes until Sophie's mom yelled, "Sophie, come to the garage right now!"

"What have you done now, Sugar?" Sophie said, giving her a side-ways glance.

When Sophie got to the garage, she was met by an unhappy looking mother, an amused-looking repairman, and the washing machine pulled away from the wall.

"Uh, what's up?" Sophie asked nervously.

The repairman laughed and held up a limp bottle brush.

Only it wasn't.

It was a tail. A squirrel tail.

"You wouldn't happen to have a cat, would you?" he teased.

Sophie glanced quickly at her mom. By the look on her mom's face, Sophie wasn't sure if she would have a cat much longer.

"I, um, I do," she meekly replied.

"Well, I do believe your cat's been keeping a little trophy case back here," the repairman said, pointing behind the washer. "I found them when I pulled the machine out to start working on it."

Sophie walked over for a peek. There, behind the appliance her mom used almost every day, was an impressive pile of squirrel tails.

"Your cat sure must love you to offer you this kind of bounty!" the man said with a chuckle.

"Well . . ." Sophie said with another quick glance at her mom, "hope-fully I can teach her to love me a little less?"

The repairman laughed, her mom rolled her eyes, and Sophie ran back to her chair.

Math homework could wait a few minutes. It was time to bring Google into this situation. Sophie picked up her phone.

"Hey, Siri, how do you teach a cat to bring you flowers instead of tails?"

PAWS & PONDER . . .

Thankfully God doesn't ask us to honor him with squirrel tails! But he does ask us to honor him with the resources he has given us. What is one way you can honor the Lord today from what he has so generously given you? How are you giving him your best?

Paws & Pray

Father, you are so generous to me. Even in seasons of want, help me remember all I have in you—life, love, forgiveness, and peace. Lord, stir my heart to gladly give back to you a portion of what you have so generously given to me. Compel me to give you my very best.

37

SOMEONE TO UNDERSTAND

Singing cheerful songs to a person with a heavy heart is like taking someone's coat in cold weather or pouring vinegar in a wound.

PROVERBS 25:20

OREO'S FEROCIOUS BARK reverberated off the walls as the Lab/husky mix ran toward the front of the house. The front door had slammed and startled him from a nap, and the protective dog was now on high alert.

Yet, the moment he realized the source of the noise was his sixteen-year-old human friend, Emily, his warning barks turned to cries of joy.

Oreo picked up his favorite tennis ball and dropped it at her feet, then darted ten feet ahead and assumed the "catch" position.

"Not today, boy," Emily said, giving his floppy black ears a scratch as she walked to her bedroom.

She collapsed on her bed, leaning against the wall of pillows she meticulously arranged every morning, then pulled out her phone and texted her mom to let her know she was home safe and sound.

Thanks sweetie, came the instant reply. *I'll be home in one hour. You okay?*

Emily rolled her eyes at her mom's question. Oh, sure, yep, all good. My dad's gone; I'm terrified to be alone; my grades are awful; and no one seems to care.

I'm fine, she texted back, adding, *See you soon.*

Emily pulled one of the pillows from behind her back and held it tightly against her chest, willing the constant ache to lessen, even if just for a moment.

The house was painfully quiet. So quiet that Emily's mind filled the void, replaying the scene at lunch today when her friend Nikki had asked her how much longer she was going to be sad about her dad's sudden death.

"Will you be over this by Homecoming?" she had asked. "I mean, I just need to know if we are still going together."

Leah, a new student this year, shot Nikki a reprimanding look. "Nikki! Seriously, that is so insensitive." Placing her hand on Emily's shoulder, she said, "You take your time grieving. I know exactly how you feel—my cat died last year."

"Your cat!" Emily choked out. Her words were indistinguishable, caught between a laugh and a hysterical sob.

Emily had lifted her tray, dumped her food in the nearest trash can, and then spent the rest of the lunch period in the restroom.

Now, as she hugged a second pillow, silent tears streamed down her face. She just needed someone to understand. Someone to sit with her. To let her talk or to sit with her in silence. To do normal things like watch a movie with or not-normal things like sorting through her dad's old T-shirts to make a memory quilt. As she wiped away her tears, two white paws appeared on the edge of her bed, followed by a black nose and two blue eyes.

Emily smiled at the three-year-old rescue dog she had received from her uncle, just before her dad's car accident. *Two months ago today.*

"Come on up, boy," Emily invited him, patting the middle of the bed.

Needing no further encouragement, Oreo leapt right up and snuggled into Emily's lap. The normally active dog released a sigh as he draped a paw across Emily's arm.

Emily stroked his left paw, tracing each nail with her finger.

"I wish you could have known Dad longer," she whispered. "He was the best."

Oreo burrowed his head further into Emily's lap as she told him all about the father she adored and how hard it was to adjust to life without him.

When Emily's mom arrived home, she found the two of them still on the bed.

"Hey, baby," Emily's mom said, kissing her daughter's forehead. "How was your day?"

Emily rubbed her hand deep into Oreo's fur and took a deep breath.

"Pretty hard," she said, glancing at her mom.

Her mom scooted in beside Emily and Oreo.

"Mine too," her mom said, wrapping her arm around Emily.

The two talked well into the night—reminiscing, crying, laughing, and at times being silent. And through it all, loyal Oreo never left their side.

PAWS & PONDER...

Allowing a hurting family member to share their thoughts; sitting with a grieving friend in silence; accompanying a distressed loved one to an appointment—simple acts which require strength, courage, and discernment. Ask God to help you be present with someone who is hurting today. And if you are hurting, ask God to send you a friend to be present with you. He may even send a friend with four paws and a tail.

Paws & Pray

Father, so often when I try to say something comforting to a friend, I end up saying the wrong thing. Please give me wisdom to know when I should speak, what I should say, and when I should simply be silently present. Shine your light of hope through me today and help me to love others well.

3 8

℞ETIRED JUDGE

Whoever tends a fig tree will eat its fruit, and he who guards

his master will be honored.

PROVERBS 27:18, ESV

BRANDON COX HAD BEEN WORKING as a K9 officer for close to a decade and knew it would take a while for him and his family to get used to his new role as sergeant. But he was most concerned with how his K9 partner, Judge, would handle the transition. Once Brandon started his new job, their assignments in the field would end.

Judge had been working the Hernando County sheriff's office in Florida for seven years—and had been working with Brandon the entire time. The dog lived and breathed his work because to the German shepherd it wasn't work at all. It was all one big game. A game he absolutely loved.

The K9 partner was a mass of energy on patrol. He was always on alert and ready to be called into action.

In fact, Judge would often get so excited while on duty that he would bark incessantly during his twelve-hour shift in the cruiser. While the barking was less than ideal in such close quarters, Brandon realized it helped Judge stay focused and ready to work at a moment's notice by providing an outlet for his pent-up energy. Thankfully, Brandon was able to quiet Judge when necessary.

Whenever it was time for Judge to get to work—whether that meant apprehending a suspect, finding a missing person, sniffing out an illegal substance, or putting himself in harm's way to protect his handler—Brandon knew his dog was ready.

Judge was simply always ready.

That quality made him a wonderful partner, but it also worried Brandon now. Would his highly trained police dog adapt well to being a house pet?

Judge was housed at Brandon's home in an outside kennel to keep him used to the elements so he could do his job well in any kind of climate. One of the perks of his retirement would be getting to move *inside* Brandon's house, where he would enjoy a comfortable climate-controlled environment. And yet, as happy as Brandon was to have his faithful partner become a member of his family, he couldn't help but wonder how the dog would respond to the dramatic changes.

Brandon had a hard time imagining Judge lying around the house all day. Would he even enjoy it? But with Brandon's new role, and Judge's age, the decision was made to retire Judge and bring in a younger dog to take his place.

The first week Judge did seem quite confused. He would pant with excitement as Brandon dressed for work, then whine and paw at the door when Brandon left without him. But it did not take long for Judge to embrace a life of ease . . . and air-conditioning in Florida.

Judge traded games like chase the suspect for games of fetch and hide-and-seek with Brandon's children. And he happily traded his kennel in the back of the police car for his soft memory foam bed.

Although his former partner is enjoying the good life of retirement, Brandon knows that if the need ever arose, Judge would not hesitate to serve, defend, and protect him and his family.

Because, after all, he's Judge.

PAWS & PONDER . . .

This proverb refers to the benefits of hard work. What are some of the rewards of hard work? Can you think of any eternal rewards of hard work? What are the "fig trees" (i.e., roles and responsibilities) God has given you to cultivate and nurture? How are you working hard at tending those?

Paws & Pray

Father, help me to work well for you. Show me how to work wisely—not for the praise of others, nor for mere financial gain, but as a testimony to my faith in you. Help me always to work with you in mind. As I work in your presence, allow others to see you in me. For you are our greatest reward.

Do not forsake wisdom, and she will protect you;
love her, and she will watch over you.

PROVERBS 4:6, NIV

39

KAREN'S BUDDY

Gracious words are like a honeycomb,

sweetness to the soul and health to the body.

PROVERBS 16:24, ESV

NOT A DAY GOES BY without Karen thinking about Buddy, her beloved Sheltie and constant companion of fifteen years.

Buddy entered Karen's life in the midst of a painful and lonely season, and the black, tan, and sable dog had quickly become her best friend—a living, breathing reminder that she wasn't alone. Buddy's unconditional affection, zeal for life, and calming presence had steadied Karen through many highs and lows and always pointed her back to the God she knew would never leave her. He served as a reminder of God's constant love and inspired Karen to live a life full of joy and laughter.

As a puppy, Buddy's energy level was more than Karen had bargained for when she agreed to take him in when his owners could no longer care for him. Desperate to give Buddy a positive outlet for his energy, Karen taught him how to catch a Frisbee. He learned quickly and loved the game. Buddy was able to catch every throw and even made Karen's bad throws look good!

Buddy also became Karen's hiking partner. At first their hikes were confined to vacations in the mountains, but when Karen moved to Tennessee, hiking became a weekly occurrence. The two delighted in exploring trails, hiking up to waterfalls, and splashing in creeks.

When Buddy and Karen weren't playing Frisbee or hiking, they were at home with Karen's African gray parrot, Bobbie. She was an intelligent and vocal bird that rapidly learned to mimic Karen's distinct whistle to call Buddy.

Poor Buddy would get quite confused when he would hear the whistle and come running, only to find Karen hadn't called him. Over the years it seemed whenever Bobbie wanted some company she would whistle for Buddy—who would always respond immediately.

But one day Bobbie whistled, and Buddy didn't come. He had become too sick with cancer to run. Soon, the disease claimed his life.

Karen was heartbroken to say goodbye to her best friend. Never before had the house, nor her heart, felt so empty. So quiet. So . . . alone.

Several days after losing him, longing to be able to once again hear the jingle of his tags, or the tip-tap of his toenails, Karen cried out, "Ah, Buddy! I miss you so much!"

Tears flowed freely down her cheeks. But just a heartbeat later, she heard

Fweet!

Then, "Buddy."

And, "Ahhh."

Bobbie! Karen held out her arm for the African gray to climb on. They whistled together for Buddy.

A whistle of goodbye.

A whistle of thanks.

A whistle that said, "You will never be forgotten."

More than two years have passed since Buddy died, but Karen still hears these three words every day: "*Fweet!* Buddy. Ahhh."

Oh, how sweet it is to hear the names of those we love.

PAWS & PONDER . . .

Does your soul long for gracious healing words? The book of Psalms assures us that God is our refuge and strength at all times, especially in times of trouble. Do you believe that promise? Is there someone in your life who needs to hear gracious words? Will you speak those words of life and hope to them today?

Paws & Pray

Father, thank you for the words you have given me. I believe these true words are life-giving, life-sustaining, and healing. Your words have been preserved for generations in order to touch my heart today. Lord, fill my mind with your words. And give me boldness to offer your words with compassion and grace to those around me.

40

ᴀ ᴘATIENT ᴿEWARD

A hot-tempered person stirs up conflict,

but the one who is patient calms a quarrel.

PROVERBS 15:18, NIV

SUNNY, A GOLDEN RETRIEVER, was lying on the family room floor—salivating. Across the room, her canine companion Chief was happily chewing a large rawhide bone. Sunny's rawhide lay beside her, untouched. She did not care for brand-new rawhides. She preferred hers well-chewed—the more slobbery the better.

Chief, a fun-loving yellow Lab, gladly surrendered sticks, toys, even food to Sunny, but he absolutely refused to abdicate his rawhide. The slightly overweight Lab had, on more than one occasion, fallen asleep with the rawhide still in his mouth.

Over the years Sunny had tried to claim Chief's well-gnawed bone. The normally docile Chief would growl and bark when she began her approach. Chief would nip at her paws when they inched a little too close. And he would cram himself into a corner, hunkering over his chew. Accepting momentary defeat, Sunny would lie down with her own bone-dry rawhide and half-heartedly begin to gnaw.

But things were about to change. Chief had developed a new obsession—squirrels. A bumper supply of acorns had drawn more squirrels than ever before to Chief's yard. And he had made it his mission to rid their property of each and every one. Chief seemed to take the presence of the bushy-tailed rodents as a personal affront and would chase them with a fierceness that surprised his human family.

Sunny preferred lizards herself, so she barely gave the squirrels a glance. However, one night when Sunny detected the glorious sound of perfectly chewed rawhide, she jumped up from the carpet and ran to the door, barking like Chief would do when he heard a squirrel.

Chief bolted to the door. The hair on the back of his neck was standing on end, and he pawed at the floor. His bark reverberated in the small room. The moment the door opened, he shot out like a rocket and ran straight to the big oak tree.

Chief ran circles around the tree. He ran back and forth along the fence. He sniffed every bush.

No squirrels.

He glanced back to find Sunny—surely she would know where the varmint was hiding.

Where was she?

Chief cocked his head to the side and raised his ears. Then he ran back into the house. Sunny was lying in the middle of the family room, happily chewing *his* perfectly slobber-basted bone.

PAWS & PONDER...

Sunny's patient self-control was rewarded with a well-chewed bone. What situation are you facing today that requires patient self-control? What could have happened if Sunny had decided to take the bone directly from Chief? What might happen if you act aggressively in your situation? Ask God for the strength to be patient as you trust him.

Paws & Pray

God, grant me the strength to be patient when my first reaction is to be hot-tempered. Being angry is easy. Lord, help me to calm a quarrel instead of starting one. Help me to trust you and your timing.

41

SIMONE THE STAR

Do not exalt yourself in the king's presence, and do not claim a
place among his great men; it is better for him to say to you, "Come
up here," than for him to humiliate you before his nobles.

PROVERBS 25:6–7, NIV

"I STILL CAN'T BELIEVE YOU are doing this." Nancy laughed as her sister, Louise, and her friend, Judy, pulled an artificial tree from its box. "It's not even Halloween yet."

Simone, Nancy's Siamese cat, fled from the room as the tree emerged.

"Yes, but you love Christmas, and we love you!" Judy declared, holding the bottom third of the tree as if it were Moses' staff.

Nancy's throat began to constrict from emotion. She rubbed the site of her latest chemo injection, grateful the nausea hadn't yet hit in full force and dismayed she was having to endure the healing poison again.

Thinking about the road ahead made her tired. She had mentioned that to Judy several days ago.

"With this new chemo schedule, I'm scared I'm not going to feel good enough to decorate for Christmas this year," she had shared over the phone.

Judy understood her friend's love of all things Christmas. However, Nancy could never have imagined that a few days later her friend would show up on her doorstep like a Christmas sugar plum fairy and declare it decorating day. Louise, who had recently come for a visit, joined right in. And within a few hours Nancy's house looked like the set of a Hallmark Christmas movie.

Her friend's kindness brought a grateful smile to her lips.

"Okay, come on, my little elves," Nancy joked. "You need a coffee break."

Leaving the top section of the tree to attach later, the women headed for the kitchen, passing Simone on the way. The playful cat made a beeline for the living room.

"So, how will she do with all the decorations?" Judy asked.

"She's a stinker," Nancy said, chuckling. "Every Christmas she acts like I put all that stuff up for her to play with."

The women chatted as they sipped steaming coffee. It all felt so normal. So familiar. So . . . healing.

"Alright, troops," Judy declared. "That tree is not going to decorate itself. Time to finish the job and stick a star on top!"

As the women walked back into the living room, they came to an abrupt halt, then broke into laughter.

Lying atop the tree—like the Christmas star—was Simone.

"Well," Louise said, "guess you don't need to put the top section on. Clearly, Simone has found the perfect napping spot."

Nancy rolled her eyes. Her kitty's antics never ceased to amuse her.

"Simone, get down!" Nancy commanded, sounding far more amused than stern.

Simone was annoyed at being disturbed. She took her time getting up, stretching and arching her back. Then with a flick of her tail, she jumped from her perch and curled up on the tree skirt.

"From being a star to being a present," Judy said, smiling.

The ladies attached the top section of the tree, filled each branch with ornaments, and secured the star. They then stood back to admire their work.

"It's perfect," Nancy whispered. "I cannot thank you enough."

It was a precious—almost sacred—moment. A moment Nancy would cherish during the difficult days ahead.

Judy looked closer at the tree.

"Is that . . ." she started, pointing at two blue eyes peeking out from the middle of the tree.

"Simone!" Nancy yelled. "Get out of that tree!"

PAWS & PONDER . . .

While Simone sought a place of honor in the tree, Nancy was honored by her friends' selfless act of kindness. How can you honor someone today?

Paws & Pray

I admit that I often want to be the star of the show, Lord, rather than following your humble example of servanthood. Jesus, you loved me so much that you left your rightful place in heaven seated next to God and came to earth to die for me. Remind me of that truth whenever I start acting like I deserve to be in the spotlight more than anyone else. I want to be a servant and show kindness to others in your name.

42

WHEN YOUR DOG TALKS . . . LISTEN

A person finds joy in giving an apt reply—
and how good is a timely word!

PROVERBS 15:23, NIV

JEN WAS FULL OF NERVOUS ENERGY about her dad's upcoming open-heart surgery. Questions swirled through her mind. Would everything go smoothly? How extensive would his rehab be? Would there be long-term consequences? *I need to find something to take my mind off Dad for a little while*, she thought. She opened the pantry and saw the plastic bin that contained all of the teaching supplies she had been using for the past four years with her preschool class at church. The bin had reached its capacity and then some. It was time to cull the contents. She began pulling out finger puppets, construction paper, and Popsicle stick signs that quickly littered the floor.

She swallowed the worry lodged in her throat. Her fingers grew cold with fear.

I am not going to start down the "what-ifs" trail, she thought as she stuffed a handful of ripped paper plates into a trash bag.

Her cell phone rang. It was her mom.

The trash bag slipped from Jen's hand.

Thankfully, her mom was just calling to confirm Jen's flight information. Jen moved into the kitchen to make herself a cup of tea while she continued the conversation. When she hung up, Jen noticed her hands were shaking.

Once again, she tried to swallow her fear.

What if?

She scrubbed the dishes in the sink.

What if?

She began rearranging the boxes in the pantry.

She heard her dog, Bailey, walk into the kitchen, but Jen was far too busy trying to avoid thinking about her dad to pay the fluffy Golden retriever much attention.

With the pantry done, Jen closed the door. She was scanning the kitchen for something else to tackle when she came to a complete stop.

Bailey was holding one of the signs from Jen's bin in her mouth: a bright orange sign with the word "Pray" written on it.

Of all the things in the bin. Of all the signs—happy face signs and sad face signs, "green means go" signs and "red means stop" signs, giant ear signs to remind the kids to listen, and big eye signs to remind them to pay attention—Bailey had picked the Pray sign.

Jen dropped to her knees in front of her dog and wrapped her arms tightly around Bailey. She began to sob, something she should have done days ago when she first learned of her dad's diagnosis.

And then, after gently taking the sign out of Bailey's mouth, Jen did what her dog suggested—she prayed.

And as she prayed, she felt fear begin to loosen its grip on her heart.

Bailey stayed with Jen the entire time she prayed on the kitchen floor. Jen prayed for strength and peace, healing and protection, joy and mercy. Then she spent time praising God and thanking him for her parents, her dad's doctors, and her friends and family who were helping in so many ways. Above all, she thanked God for loving her so much that he sent her a message through her dog.

A dog who had given her just the right word at just the right moment.

PAWS & PONDER . . .

Can you recall a time someone shared a timely word with you? How did that word help you? Is there someone in your life today who might need a word of encouragement? How could you speak words of life, grace, and hope to that person today?

Paws & Pray

Lord, thank you for speaking to me through your Word and through the words you give others to say to me. Give me the courage to speak words of life to those around me. Open my eyes to see the needs of others. And then open my mouth and my hands so that I might help to meet their needs as much as possible.

43

OH, WHAT LOVE

A friend loves at all times,

and a brother is born for adversity.

PROVERBS 17:17, ESV

AMY'S HEART RACED when she saw the flatbed truck coming down the two-lane country road.

"Jaxson! Buddy!" she called, frantically trying to locate her two dogs who had run out of the house while she unloaded the groceries. She scanned her yard, the neighbor's yard, and the overgrown hedgerow behind her property.

"Oh, Lord," she whispered, her stomach lurching at the thought of her two Golden retrievers running into traffic and being hit.

Rain was coming down in torrents, and drivers would not be able to see, let alone brake for a couple of dogs running like mad across the road. Tears and rain streamed down Amy's face as she sprinted across yards, between homes, and down the street. She decided she could cover a wider area in her car, so she ran home, got in her car, and began to slowly drive down street after street.

"Buddy! Jaxson!"

Amy's throat burned and her voice was getting hoarse, but still she called for them. *Why didn't I make sure the door was tightly closed?* Finally she spotted the dogs, sniffing and frolicking in a neighbor's flower garden, oblivious to her panic.

"Buddy! Jaxson! Stop!"

They lifted their heads for a moment and stared at Amy, then quickly ran off again. *How will I ever get them back?* These were her constant companions, her fur-babies. Her own . . . personal therapy dogs. For years her dogs had helped her cope with PTSD, a condition resulting from early abuse at the hands of those who should have protected her. Along with providing companionship and protection, Buddy and Jaxson had taught her how to trust again.

She had to save them.

She needed a different tactic.

"Hey guys, wanna go for a ride? Come on, let's go for a ride!" she called out.

That caught their attention. They stopped running.

She called to them again, inviting them on a ride—a ride they knew usually meant walks in the park, burgers at the drive-through, or ice cream.

The two dogs bounded toward the car. Amy opened the back door for them, laughing and praising them as they barreled onto the back seat. Their tails were soggy, and they were getting mud all over everything.

But Amy could not have been happier.

She didn't care that they were dirty or had disobeyed. All that mattered was that they were safe and sound.

Amy realized that her desperate effort to save her unruly, filthy, obstinate dogs was nothing compared to Jesus' willingness to save her unruly, filthy, obstinate heart. She was overwhelmed by the depth of Jesus' love for her. Yes, Amy would have done anything—even run in front of a speeding flatbed truck—to save her dogs. But Jesus *did* everything, dying on a rugged cross, to save her.

"Oh, what love," Amy whispered prayerfully, as two muddy companions licked her happily.

PAWS & PONDER...

In spite of Jaxson and Buddy's disobedience, Amy still loved them and wanted them to come home. Do you ever struggle with feeling too dirty or too guilty for God to love you? You are his child, and you are loved with a love that cannot end. Ask the Lord to whisper those truths to your heart and to help you accept them.

Paws & Pray

Lord, thank you for loving me at all times, even when I feel so far away from you. Your all-encompassing love is difficult to comprehend—you pursue me when I am going my own way, forgive me when I feel unforgivable, and see me as your master-piece when I can only see a mess. God, help me to become more aware of your love daily.

Doing wrong is fun for a fool, but living wisely brings pleasure to the sensible.

PROVERBS 10:23

44

ANNIE'S NEW BED

A wise woman builds her home, but a foolish woman

tears it down with her own hands.

PROVERBS 14:1

GREG AND MEGAN WERE TAKEN ABACK when they walked into their central Florida home. The floors of the kitchen and family room were covered in what looked like mounds of snow.

"Um . . . is that—" Megan began, stopping herself before asking the question. There was no way it had snowed inside their house, in the middle of summer, in Florida.

Greg grabbed a handful of the soft white substance.

"Annie," he called. "Come here."

Greg and Megan's seven-year-old corgi emerged from the back bedroom of their ranch-style home. She walked tentatively, as if she were stepping on eggshells, with her head nearly touching the floor and her tail drooping behind her.

"Annie, what did you do?" Megan asked.

The couple quickly began taking inventory.

The sofa was still intact.

The pillows were all in place.

Their master-bedroom door was still shut.

And Annie's toy bin was filled only with tennis balls and rubber toys. She wasn't allowed to have any stuffed toys because she always destroyed them. Every time Megan was tempted to buy a cute stuffed toy, Greg would tell her she might as well just hand the dog the cash and let her eat the money instead.

What had Annie destroyed?

"In here," Greg called from the back bedroom.

There, in the middle of the floor, were the shredded remnants of Annie's brand-new dog bed. It had been an expensive orthopedic bed Megan had purchased after Annie's last check-up when the vet mentioned his concern about Annie's stiff joints. The vet had recommended a supplement and a quality supportive bed.

Last night was the first time Annie had slept on the bed. And Megan felt confident the splurge was worth it.

Until now.

"Ugh, Annie! That bed was supposed to help you feel better," Megan groaned. "And it was *so* expensive . . ."

Megan and Greg cleaned up the debris before turning in for the night.

Days later, when Annie started limping after playing at the park, Megan went to the pet store to buy another, less expensive bed.

Annie slept all night on the memory foam bed.

She napped on it the next day.

After the third day without a shredding incident, Megan told Greg, "I think we have a winner!"

Until she came home that evening to more piles of foam.

"Oh, my word, Annie," Megan said. "Why do you insist on destroying your beds? I'm only trying to make you comfortable."

As Megan filled the trash with chunks of foam, her mind began to race, searching for solutions. *Do they make dog beds from Kevlar? Can you coat one in Teflon? How can I teach Annie to stop chewing her bed so she can enjoy its long-term benefits?*

Just then, Annie came bounding around the corner—a chunk of foam held firmly between her teeth. Clearly wanting to play with her new "toy," Annie play-bowed to Megan.

"Oh, Annie," Megan chuckled, grabbing a treat from the counter and trading the morsel for the foam. "Maybe I should see if dog beds come wrapped in chain mail!"

PAWS & PONDER...

In what ways might a foolish woman tear down her house? Why do you think the phrase "with her own hands" was included in the proverb? In what ways does a wise woman build her house? What else might the term *house* mean in the verse? How can you guard yourself against tearing down your house with your own hands?

Paws & Pray

Lord, so often I choose temporary pleasure over long-lasting benefits or eternal rewards. I get so caught up running after the things of this world that I forget you are the only one who can truly satisfy the deepest longing of my heart. God, fill my mind with an awareness of you so that I can be strong when I am tempted.

45

฿RILEY'S GIFT

My child, hold on to your wisdom and insight.
Never let them get away from you.

PROVERBS 3:21, GNT

BRILEY STUDIED the room closely. The ten-year-old German shepherd was assessing the needs of the group gathered there—which residents needed her immediate attention and comfort and which ones could wait until later.

Her owner, April, watched in amazement, even though she had seen this happen every time they came to the nursing home. It was her dog's MO, an inherent gentleness and awareness of people's emotional needs that April had noticed from the time Briley was a puppy. April had enrolled Briley in the necessary certification classes to become a volunteer therapy dog. And now, five years later, Briley was quite the therapy dog expert.

The community room was full of men and women eager to pet one of the five visiting therapy dogs. April saw Briley crane her neck, sniff the air, and tilt her head side to side. *She's looking for a specific person.*

As April held the leash loosely, Briley slowly began moving through the crowd, stopping for quick pats, laying her head in a lap for a moment, offering her paw in a canine handshake.

After several minutes, Briley zeroed in on one particular person—a woman sitting off in a corner by herself.

April could barely see the woman's face because her head was bowed. When she looked up, her eyes were vacant.

The woman was physically in the room but clearly far away at the same time.

Briley walked purposefully to the woman. Sitting at her feet, Briley laid her large head on the colorful afghan covering the woman's lap.

Suddenly, April heard the woman gasp, startled by the unexpected visitor.

Briley kept her head on the woman's lap and turned on the charm, her deep brown eyes riveted on the woman's.

And then it happened. April detected the faintest hint of a smile on the woman's face.

She placed her wrinkled, fragile hands against Briley's forehead.

The two sat—canine and human—staring at each other. The connection between them was so strong April could almost feel it.

As the other therapy dogs made their rounds that day, giving and receiving affection, Briley stayed with the woman.

After several minutes, the nursing home director approached April.

"That was kind of you to send your dog over to Ms. Ida," she said softly. "She has been lost since her husband died last week. It's so good to see her smile."

"It was all Briley's idea," April said, still amazed at her dog's keen sense of a person's emotions.

How did Briley know Ms. Ida needed her today?

When Briley lifted her head to receive a kiss from Ms. Ida, April nearly started crying.

For the rest of the visit, Ms. Ida talked to Briley, her right hand never leaving the German shepherd's head.

Briley sat in rapt attention, providing the simple yet powerful gift of quiet companionship.

PAWS & PONDER...

What practical steps can you take to become more insightful? Briley's actions were very purposeful. What does purposefulness have to do with holding on to wisdom and insight? What situation are you facing today that would benefit from assessing your options before making a decision? Take a few minutes to ask God to fill you with everything you need to accomplish his will.

Paws & Pray

Father God, you are the author and supplier of wisdom. I look to you to provide me with insight on how I can live more effectively for you. Lord, help me cling to the wisdom you give me and use that knowledge to comfort others.

46

WHO TOOK THE BALL?

Do not plot harm against your neighbor, who lives trustfully near you.

PROVERBS 3:29, NIV

THE MOMENT THE ENERGETIC TERRIER MIX named Jack noticed Tyler and Trevor were home from school, he sprinted across the backyard in record time. The fifteen-pound dog jumped from one boy to the next, desperate for a game of catch.

"Okay, okay, Jack," eleven-year-old Trevor said, laughing at the small dog's enthusiasm. "We will play with you."

Tyler, a year older than his brother, hunted for a tennis ball in the yard.

"Found one!" he yelled, holding the ball up in victory, before throwing it low to the ground.

Jack bounded after the ball, making quick work of retrieving his fuzzy green toy. Tyler threw it again and Jack raced after it.

"Hey, I want to throw it!" Trevor whined.

"Go find your own ball," Tyler shot back.

Trevor huffed and began combing the yard for another ball. "I can't find one. There's no more out here."

Tyler tossed a ball high in the air to Jack. "Trevor, you can never find anything. Look under the deck."

The deck? Snakes live under there!

Trevor turned just in time to see Jack catch a ball in midair! *Tyler can't have all the fun with Jack!* Jealousy propelled him past his fear. Trevor hesitated, then peeked under the deck and spied several tennis balls.

But there was more stuff. A *lot* more. Trevor spotted a small soccer ball, gardening gloves, a sandbox shovel, and a little kid's tennis shoe!

"What are those doing under here?" Trevor asked aloud, scrambling under the deck.

By this time Tyler had come to investigate what had captured his brother's attention. Trevor pushed the soccer ball into the yard. "Hey, this is nice," Tyler said. "Whose is it, and why is it under here?"

Trevor crawled out into the sunshine with his finds, looked at Tyler, and shrugged. "Don't know." The boys looked around their yard. Jack's high-pitched bark signaled his growing impatience. Trevor picked up a tennis ball from the pile and threw it.

As the tan and white dog raced after the ball, Tyler and Trevor heard, "Hey! Dat's my ball!" Bennett, the four-year-old boy who lived behind them, was standing by the picket fence.

Tyler looked at the blue and white ball.

He started to walk it over to the youngster, but stopped to grab the shovel, gloves, and shoe.

"Are these yours too?" Tyler asked, extending the items to the boy.

Two chubby hands reached for the ball. "The glubs are Mama's, but the shubel and shoe is mines."

Tyler handed Bennett the ball before sliding the other items through the fence slats into Bennett's yard and setting them on the ground.

"Why you have my ball?" the little boy asked, his eyebrows wrinkled in accusation.

Jack ran to Tyler, dropping a tennis ball at his feet.

Bennett reached his arm through the wood slats. "Hi, doggie! Come, doggie!"

"Bennett, did you give Jack your ball?" Tyler asked as Trevor approached.

Blond curls bounced as the boy shook his head. "No doggie's ball; Bennett's ball," he said, scowling at the dog.

Trevor walked several feet away, his gaze sweeping the ground near the fence.

"Ty, over here," he called to his brother.

As Tyler got closer, he saw a terrier-sized tunnel from their yard into the neighbors'.

"Jack!" Tyler scolded. "You little thief. You've been stealing Bennett's toys, haven't you!"

As if the dog knew he had been caught, Jack bolted from the fence and ran straight to the back door.

"You can run, but Mom's still gonna find out!" Trevor shouted.

"Sorry, Bennett," Tyler said. "We won't let Jack take your ball any-more, okay? Our dad will fix the hole."

Tyler's apology went completely unnoticed by the little boy who had become distraught when Jack skedaddled. "No, doggie! Come back, dog-gie!" Bennett cried, throwing his ball over the fence. "Get ball, doggie!"

And with one leap from the deck, Jack happily obeyed.

PAWS & PONDER...

Take a moment and consider how you might extend kindness to your neighbors this week. Perhaps you could take them a meal, write an encouraging note, or offer to watch their kids for an evening. Or consider a project to serve your larger com-munity. Brainstorm with your family or a Bible study group to find ways to serve your neighbors, and in doing so, help shine the hope and love of Jesus even further.

Paws & Pray

Lord, in the hustle and bustle of my day, it is so easy to rush right past my neigh-bors. Help me slow down enough to see the needs of those around me. Give me the resources to meet their needs.

47

WISE EDDIE

The wise are cautious and avoid danger;

fools plunge ahead with reckless confidence.

PROVERBS 14:16

IF IT'S TRUE THAT CATS have nine lives, then Eddie was on his eighth. Babette had noticed the young cat wandering in the neighborhood, so she began setting food out for him. That simple act turned into a month of caring for him, including several trips to the vet. Thirty-five days and countless "lost cat" flyers later, his owner finally contacted her and reclaimed his cat.

Two years later, Babette got a call from the vet saying the clinic had her cat. "I don't understand," she said, thoroughly confused. She learned that the cat had been found more than three miles from her house, again wandering the streets. He had been microchipped when Babette was caring for him, so her phone number was the one on file. Unable to track down the cat's owner, Babette decided to keep the cat who had acquired several names along the way.

The vet called him Caramel Macchiato. His first owner said his name was Stripes. Babette's sons referred to him by a variety of nicknames. But once he officially became their family's cat, Babette renamed him Eddie.

She had no idea why. He just seemed like an Eddie.

Eddie seemed to adapt fairly quickly to his new home, where he never lacked companionship—neither human nor animal.

Babette and her husband, Bob, were avid animal lovers committed to rescuing creatures in need. Not surprisingly, they had collected a menagerie of pets over the years.

Things were going smoothly . . . and then Harley became part of their family.

Harley, a German shepherd/collie mix, was rescued not long after giving birth to a litter. However, her puppies were never found. The loss clearly affected Harley. She barely ate anything, and she became more and more lethargic.

Babette's heart went out to the despondent dog.

Weeks later a small chihuahua named Willie joined their small pack. Instantly Harley perked up. She even began to mother the little guy. She cleaned him, scolded him when he got out of line, and tucked him in for the night by wrapping her tail around him. Harley had clearly adopted Willie as her puppy.

She was the definition of gentleness to the little dog.

But that was not the case with poor Eddie.

As gentle as Harley was with Willie, she was aggressive toward Eddie.

Maybe Harley had been attacked by a feral cat when the dog was abandoned. Whatever her history was with cats, Harley decided her mission was to terrorize Eddie now. Between ferocious barking, incessant chasing, and a frightening nip, Harley made it clear she would not tolerate Eddie's presence anywhere near her.

Babette tried to play the role of peacemaker and gatekeeper as best she could. Thankfully, she didn't have to assume the role for long.

Eddie quickly figured out how to protect his ninth life, by taking up residence in the basement, which was off-limits to Harley.

From his sanctuary in the basement, Eddie could hear the sound of Harley's crate being closed and latched. The moment the shepherd mix was secured upstairs, Eddie would quietly venture to the first floor. And if Harley was invited to spend the night in one of Babette's sons' rooms, the moment the bedroom door was shut, Eddie wandered the halls of the house in peace.

Eddie the cat, with his many names and past residences, had figured out how to avoid the dichotomy that was Harley.

Babette knew Eddie's street smarts—and house smarts—would extend his life, and hopefully even give him back one or two.

PAWS & PONDER...

Do you find yourself tempted to do something without thinking instead of using caution? Can you recall a time when you plunged ahead with reckless confidence? What were the results? How might you use caution and discernment in a situation you are facing today?

Paws & Pray

Father, thank you for giving me a mind that can carefully think through things and weigh the consequences of my actions. Help me to cultivate those gifts by spending time with you and your Word. If I am headed into danger, let me hear your voice calling me back to you and to your will.

48

℞UBY'S ℘AW

Whoever conceals his transgressions will not prosper,

but he who confesses and forsakes them will obtain mercy.

PROVERBS 28:13, ESV

WHEN DONNA ADOPTED three-year-old Ruby, she had no idea how much the black Lab would teach her about her own relationship with God.

The first time Donna took Ruby for a walk, the black Lab bounded out the door like Tigger showing off for Winnie-the-Pooh. Ruby couldn't get enough of her new neighborhood. She wanted to sniff every tree, greet every person, and chase every squirrel. Donna and Ruby walked for quite a while before turning around and heading back home. About ten minutes away from her house, Donna noticed Ruby was limping slightly. She mentally retraced their course, trying to remember if Ruby had done anything that might have caused an injury. Other than jumping up against a tree while chasing a squirrel, Donna couldn't think of anything Ruby might have done to hurt her leg.

When they returned home, Donna watched as Ruby limped around the kitchen. She was definitely favoring her front right leg, so Donna massaged it.

Ruby didn't pull the leg back in pain when Donna touched it. She just held her paw slightly off the ground.

Donna gently turned Ruby's paw over and spotted the problem: A small chunk of gravel was lodged between two of the pads.

"Oh, poor baby," Donna said soothingly, gently removing the stone.

Ruby put her paw down and immediately ran to get her favorite stuffed toy.

Several days later at the end of another walk, Donna again noticed Ruby limping.

This time Donna checked Ruby's paw first and, sure enough, once again a small stone was lodged between the pads.

To Donna's amazement, from that time on, whenever Ruby would get something caught in her paw, she would come to a complete stop, lift her paw, and wait for Donna to clean it.

Watching her dog hold her paw up—holding out what was hurting her—to Donna, was like hearing God whisper to Donna's heart, "Hold your hurts out to me."

Whether her hurt was caused by loss, other people, or her own sin, Donna knew God never intended for her to limp through life carrying a hurt she was never meant to carry.

With every walk she and Ruby took, Donna began listing her hurts, pain, and sin, and offering them up to God.

Confessing them to him.

Waiting on him.

Trusting him.

And then walking with him once again—restored, forgiven, and whole.

PAWS & PONDER...

Are you quick to bring your hurts to God? Quick to confess your sin? Or do you tend to limp through life, fighting through the pain? Trying to ignore your sin? Take a few minutes right now to hold your heart out to the Lord. Show him your hurts, invite him into your pain, and confess your sin to him. When you confess and admit your needs, he will provide mercy and healing.

Paws & Pray

Lord, help me to trust you. And in trusting you, I ask you to give me the strength I need to run toward you and not away from you. Whisper in my heart and remind me to hold my hurts out to you, allowing you to make me new.

The righteous care for the needs of their animals.

PROVERBS 12:10, NIV

49

CHIEF'S STRONG TOWER

The name of the Lord is a strong tower;

the righteous man runs into it and is safe.

PROVERBS 18:10, ESV

BOOM! The house shook from the roar of thunder, and the lightning put on an impressive strobe light show. The storm had quickly intensified from a summer shower to a powerful thunderstorm. Bill and Julie slammed the door behind them after bringing the last of the furniture cushions in from the screened porch, so the driving rain wouldn't soak them.

Another loud clap of thunder was followed by a white blur zipping from the family room, through the kitchen, and into the back bedroom.

"What was that?" Julie asked.

Her husband of forty years laughed. "Well, it was either a bolt of lightning indoors, or it was Chief."

The yellow Lab named Chief had stolen Bill's heart from the moment they met six months earlier at the breeder's house. The retired police officer, who now taught criminal justice, had picked out his dog's name years before ever finding his companion. Chief was everything Bill had hoped for—loving, playful, loyal, and easy to train.

But he was also completely terrified of thunder.

The first time Chief heard thunder, he had jumped from his bed to Bill's lap in one leap and stayed there until the skies cleared. Of course, Chief quickly outgrew Bill's lap.

As his size increased, Chief began destroying his toys whenever thunder rumbled.

Like the stormy evening Bill and his wife, Julie, arrived home to find Chief in a frenzy, gutting his favorite stuffed animal and scattering its insides all over his crate.

However, the storm blowing through their neighborhood now was the worst they'd had in a while, so Bill decided to go check on his dog.

I'm sure I can still get him in my lap if I need to, Bill determined, walking down the hall that Chief had just sped through.

"Chief, buddy, come here, boy!" Bill called.

Chief didn't make a sound.

"Chiefy, you're okay, bud. Come here."

Silence.

Bill walked into the guest room and looked for Chief. *Where is he?* And then Bill saw a tail and rear end sticking out from under the bed. Chief had shimmied as far under the bed as he could get.

Bill smiled, then lay beside his trembling friend.

"Good job, buddy," he said, soothingly. "You found a good safe place."

Chief stared at Bill as he army-crawled closer to the man he would follow anywhere. Together, man and dog were secure with their heads under the bed until the storm passed.

Chief never did outgrow his fear of thunder. In fact, ten years later, an intense clap of thunder made Julie gasp as she was preparing dinner. Seconds later, Chief ran past her and down the back hall as fast as his arthritic legs would take him.

Bill emerged from his office and began searching for his best friend. At close to a hundred pounds, Chief hadn't fit under the bed in quite a while. But clearly Chief did not know that. Bill laughed when he found his dog in the bedroom at the end of the hallway. Chief's entire body was sticking out from under the bed, with only his head tucked under the bed skirt.

"Oh, Chief," Bill said, carefully trying not to twist his own arthritic knee as he lay down on his stomach beside his dog. "You're still safe here, buddy. And I've still gotcha."

PAWS & PONDER...

Where do you run when the storms of life come? Where is your strong tower? Is your safe place a temporary solution? Or a lasting tower? Do you panic and get frantic? Chief learned exactly where to go at the first sign of a storm. Consider how different you might weather the next storm if you were to run straight into the arms of the everlasting, immoveable God. He is always there—always waiting for you to come. Thankfully, you can never outgrow his arms.

Paws & Pray

Father, I confess that I often run to flimsy towers when storms come. Help me run to you instead. I believe you are my strong tower, my refuge, and my strength. Hold me tightly through each and every storm I face, Lord. I do trust you but I pray you will increase my trust even more.

50

ĐON'T ƐAT ȚHE ĐRAGON!

The righteous choose their friends carefully,

but the way of the wicked leads them astray.

PROVERBS 12:26, NIV

CAPTAIN TIM, a bright tangerine-colored bearded dragon, was adjusting nicely to his new home in a forty-gallon terrarium that Michael kept in his room. The thirteen-year-old had wanted a bearded dragon ever since he had seen one years before on an episode of *The Crocodile Hunter*. Michael had been saving money for years to buy one with all its necessary paraphernalia.

The reptile was definitely an exotic addition to the family's pets—Sadie, the Golden retriever, and Whiskers, the calico cat. At first neither Sadie nor Whiskers was allowed in Michael's room while Captain Tim adjusted to his new home. But when the bearded dragon became used to his new environment, the larger animals were allowed back in. Captain Tim's tank was covered with a well-secured heavy-duty screen, so Michael felt sure his friend was safe.

Michael took his responsibilities seriously as he cared for Captain Tim. He kept the terrarium clean, provided Tim with an ample supply of fresh water and crickets, and ensured the temperature and humidity were at optimum levels. He gave Tim a basking rock, a vine for climbing, and a hollow log for hiding. In the afternoons, Michael would let Tim sit on his shoulder while he did homework. And in the evenings, he would play his guitar for the dragon before he went to sleep.

Once a month Michael also gave Tim a soak in the tub—something he did when his younger sisters weren't around or they would insist on lining their Barbie dolls up on the side of the tub to watch the "dragon show."

One day, while Michael was sitting on the side of the tub watching Captain Tim, Sadie barged through the half-open bathroom door. Without warning, the Golden jumped into the shallow water and licked Tim's back. Captain Tim let out a hissing sound and then flattened his body in the water.

"Sadie, no!" Michael screamed, jumping up and trying to pull the dog out of the tub.

The dog play-bowed to Tim, begging the dragon to frolic with her. Captain Tim raised his head and hissed again. His attempt at dominance only enticed Sadie to play.

Just as Sadie lunged toward the reptile with jaws open, ready to scoop him up in her mouthy version of tag, Michael grabbed Tim. He quickly wrapped the bearded dragon in a little fleece towel, then sprinted to his room and shut the door.

"Tim, I'm so sorry," he said. "Sadie was just saying hi. She wants to be your friend."

Michael inspected Tim thoroughly to make sure he wasn't injured, gingerly placed the reptile on his basking rock, and closed the lid to the terrarium. Suddenly, Sadie scratched at the bedroom door, followed by several barks. Tim's head turned in high alert.

"Sadie's a nice dog," Michael assured the bearded dragon, "but it's probably best not to be friends with someone who can eat you."

PAWS & PONDER...

What do you believe makes a good friend? What are some of the dangers of not choosing friends carefully? How can you love others while being careful about who you invite into your life as friends?

Paws & Pray

Father, help me to be a good friend and to choose my friends wisely. Give me eyes to see any toxic relationships I have, and give me strength and courage to end them. Lord, thank you for being my best friend of all.

51

TRAVELING WITH FREEDOM

It is pleasant to see dreams come true, but fools refuse to

turn from evil to attain them.

PROVERBS 13:19

WHEN JOE HAWLEY ADOPTED his boxer, Freedom, he was certain he was living the dream—in this case, his second one. His first one had been a wild ride, but it was behind him now. Maybe to some people, giving up that dream hadn't been Hawley's best move.

Since he had been a kid, all Joe wanted to do was be an NFL player. That was his idea of the American Dream. And then it happened. He was drafted in 2010 by the Atlanta Falcons. After five seasons, he followed the Falcons' offensive coordinator to Tampa Bay. He played his position as lineman intensely because he was grateful for the opportunity. But it was taking a toll on his body and his psyche. Injuries began to sideline him, and he started experiencing anxiety and stress—fearing who he was without the game that dominated his life and worrying about what would happen to him when football was gone. So before the front office could make a decision for him, Hawley walked away from his career.

Now he was living the American Dream Take Two.

Hawley gave away most of his possessions, bought a van, and had it customized as a full-time home on the road. Freed from the pursuit of more—more money, more possessions, more fame—he traveled the country with Freedom at his side.

He had met her at an animal shelter in Florida. The two-year-old boxer was cowering and shaking in her enclosure. Joe needed a companion and she deserved to be freed.

Freedom was Joe's new dream, and it became his new dog's name.

Freedom instantly took to life on the open road, becoming the best traveling companion Joe could have asked for. She has been a constant reminder for Joe that less can truly be more. All Freedom needs to be happy is some food, water, Joe, and the occasional open field where she can run.

For the two of them, it's living with less to experience more.

Their adventures are documented on ManVanDogBlog on Facebook, Instagram, and YouTube videos, inspiring thousands of people to stop and consider what will make their life fuller and better.[2]

PAWS & PONDER . . .

What are your dreams? What are you doing to pursue them? Do you feel the need to pursue a life of more? Or are you actively trying to live with less? Is there something you need to do in order to embrace the dream God has given you?

Paws & Pray

Lord, you are the giver of dreams. Thank you for the dreams you have placed in my heart. Give me the courage and ability to reach for those dreams and the discernment to let go of others if that is needed for me to embrace the plan you have for me.

---

[2] I enjoyed researching this story about Joe Hawley and his boxer, Freedom. I used two main sources: https://blog.theanimalrescuesite.greatergood.com/joe-freedom-travel/and https://www.youtube.com/channel/UCH-fGbXb-BCZ2d7c1LIXjdg.

52

WHERE ARE THE CATS?

Do you like honey? Don't eat too much, or it will make you sick!

PROVERBS 25:16

JENNIFER SHOOK THE RAIN off her umbrella, then leaned it against the side of her pet-sitting client's house. She retrieved a key from her pocket, unlocked the front door, and entered the dimly lit foyer.

"Plato . . . Aristotle . . . Socrates . . . Jack," she called to the cats she had been taking care of all week.

No response.

"Here kitty, kitties. Where are you?"

Jennifer looked in the kitchen where Plato liked to play with the rug. She peeked in the family room expecting to see Aristotle and Jack wrestling with the curtains. She walked to Socrates's favorite hiding spot in the dining room and looked under the table where the tabby would often nap after eating.

No cats anywhere.

She tried not to panic as she mentally retraced her steps from the night before. She had come by at seven and was greeted by four attention-seeking cats. She had cleaned the litter box, scooped kibble in their bowls, put down fresh water, and then played with them for a few minutes. All four had been happy, healthy, and accounted for when she left. *What could have happened?*

She checked the back door. It was securely locked. And all the bedroom doors in the home were closed.

"Kitties?" she yelled, somewhat frantically.

Suddenly, a muffled sound reached her straining ears. But it wasn't a meow or a hiss. *Was that a moan?*

Jennifer willed the sound to repeat again.

There! It was coming from the laundry room.

Jennifer ran to the room and stopped in the doorway. There, lying on the tiled floor, were all four cats—each sprawled with legs fully extended and with the roundest bellies she had ever seen.

"What in the world?" Jennifer spoke softly and knelt down to pet Jack.

The Russian Blue was sleeping in a pile of kibble. Jennifer's gaze followed a path of dry food to their source—an open and empty container lying on its side. Jennifer racked her brain. She thought she had closed the lid securely after feeding the cats last night. Either her memory was going, or the cats had somehow managed to pop off the lid and then feasted nonstop on their plunder.

Jennifer moved to Plato, running her hand over his distended belly. A feline deep moan escaped his half-open mouth, making his long whiskers vibrate.

"Oh, you guys!" Jennifer chastised. "How much did you eat?"

Socrates opened one eye and looked at her.

"Just couldn't stop, huh, buddy?"

The spotted cat closed his eye.

"You okay, Aristotle?" she asked, bending down to scratch him between his ears.

The tan and white cat raised his head for a moment, before it thudded back to the floor.

After making sure the food-coma patients had fresh water and jotting down the name of the food she needed to buy to refill the container, Jennifer let herself out and drove back home.

When she arrived, she took off her boots and coat, then headed straight for the bowl of Christmas candy on the kitchen counter. Instinctively, she grabbed a heaping handful on her way by. But suddenly a picture of four passed-out gluttonous cats passed through her mind.

She dropped all but a single piece back into the bowl. "Maybe I should just have one today," she said to herself, chuckling.

PAWS & PONDER...

It's been said that "too much of anything can be bad." Do you agree with this statement? Can you think of an example from your own life when too much of a good thing caused a problem? What do you need to "put back in the bowl" today in order to maintain balance and moderation?

Paws & Pray

Lord, there are so many good and worthwhile things competing for my time, my attention, and my resources. Please grant me greater self-control so I know when to say "enough"—even to good things. Help me to choose you first and then trust you to help me balance the rest.

5 3

A FUTURE HOPE

There is surely a future hope for you, and your hope will not be cut off.

PROVERBS 23:18, NIV

THE DOG'S PITIFUL CRIES pierced Ruth's heart. While she loved volunteering at the animal shelter and spending time with the dogs, she hated having to put them back in their enclosures. She knelt down, getting closer to the lovable beagle mix who was jumping at the chain-link fence that separated him from the play area.

"Oh, buddy," she said, pulling a tasty consolation prize from her pocket. "I know it's hard to go back inside for now, but trust me, one day soon you will forget all about this place."

The dog she had nicknamed Moonpie swallowed the treat in one gulp, then pawed her hand for more.

Ruth chuckled, "Well, at least you can be bribed."

With two more treats in her hand, she led the dog back to his four-by-four enclosure and secured the door. Moonpie took his treats and retreated to the back corner of the space and lay down, his head resting between his paws.

Ruth sat crossed-legged on the cement floor in front of the kennel and put her fingers through the openings in the barrier between her and the dog.

"Okay, here's the deal, Moonpie," she began, as if talking to a friend and not a downcast dog. "You aren't happy here. And I get that. It's loud and smelly and not at all comfortable. I wouldn't like it here either. But the truth is, this place is better than the streets where you came from. You're safe here. You're being cared for and fed."

As if sensing his starring role in her monologue, Moonpie walked over and stuck his black nose through the opening where Ruth's fingers were. She rubbed his snout.

"So you see," she said adjusting her legs, "even though this isn't great, it's a better place for you. But here's the good news: This place is nothing like where you are going."

Ruth had been ecstatic to learn Moonpie would be going home with his forever family in a few days. "Where you are going is going to be amazing. I think they even have kids for you to play with! Before you know it, you'll forget all about this place. Soon you are going to know happiness like you have never imagined because you will be home." Ruth's voice caught on the last word.

As Moonpie licked Ruth's palm, she thought of her grandmother who had just been admitted into full-time hospice care. Ruth loved her deeply and admired her rock-solid faith.

"Oh, Ruth," her grandmother had said from her bed in the hospice facility. "I don't like this place. There are too many people. Too much noise. And I'm just very tired."

The look on her grandmother's face had left Ruth heartbroken and searching for words of comfort. What could she have possibly said?

But now, as Ruth gently stroked the side of Moonpie's face, the words she had just spoken to the dog seemed to apply to her grandmother too. In the midst of the noisy animal shelter, it was almost as if she could overhear God whispering to her grandmother, "*In just a little while, you will forget all about this place. Soon you are going to know happiness like you have never imagined. My beloved child, soon you will be home.*"

PAWS & PONDER...

"My hope is built on nothing less than Jesus' blood and righteousness." These lyrics from a familiar hymn proclaim a powerful truth. What does it mean to build your hope on Jesus' blood and righteousness? How does the promise of a future hope help you endure a difficult season?

JENNIFER MARSHALL BLEAKLEY

Paws & Pray

Lord, sometimes I am overwhelmed by all the heartache, pain, and brokenness in this world. It makes it difficult for me to feel hopeful. And yet, you promise to never leave me or forsake me. You promise me life and love and peace through your Son. Help me to trust in you—the only source of true hope. I look forward to the day when I will be with you forever.

Drink water from your own cistern,
flowing water from your own well.

PROVERBS 5:15, ESV

54

A HOUSE FOR SQUEEKER

A house is built by wisdom and becomes strong through good sense. Through knowledge its rooms are filled with all sorts of precious riches and valuables.

PROVERBS 24:3-4

WHEN SKEETER, Bonnie's Chinese crested dog, carefully placed a baby squirrel at her feet, she had no idea how much her life was going to change.

Bonnie quickly surmised that the little squirrel—who appeared to be only weeks old—had fallen from its nest. Fearing the worst, Bonnie was amazed to discover the squirrel seemed just fine, albeit a little wet from Skeeter's kisses.

After some online research—and after discovering there were no wildlife rehabilitation centers nearby—Bonnie decided she would care for the rescued squirrel until it was able to be released back into the wild. Having cared for baby birds, abandoned bunnies, and rescued goats before, she felt confident she was up to the task.

She named the female squirrel Squeeker and was quite happy to take care of her—which meant bottle-feeding, snuggling, and introducing her to her new environment.

Squeeker grew rapidly, soon forgoing formula for solid food, and snuggle time for exploring expeditions—first in the house, then in a tall outdoor cage, then to the freedom of the great outdoors. During the time Bonnie cared for Squeeker, she loved watching the squirrel's silly and often amusing antics as she shimmied up curtains, learned how to open pecans, and discovered the joys of nesting with toilet paper. However, Bonnie's husband, Jeff, was not quite as amused, because as cute as Squeeker was, she was equally destructive in their bathroom.

Squeeker's favorite place to nest was a little cranny in the 1920s farmhouse bathroom. The opening—which Bonnie surmised had inadvertently been created during a bathroom remodel—was exactly squirrel-sized. Squeeker quickly claimed it as her own and began filling it with things she treasured—a bobby pin, a tube of lipstick, a juicy grape, a piece of jewelry, an almond, and a ton of toilet paper. Things that Bonnie wouldn't have thought special or important became precious treasures to Squeeker.

Periodically, Bonnie would clean out Squeeker's squirrel house so that the little tidbits of food didn't start to smell, but Squeeker would quickly fill it back up.

Day after day as Bonnie watched her little squirrel hunt for new and exciting treasures, Bonnie began to realize the importance of celebrating and honoring those things—mementos and trinkets—that are important to us, even the ones that don't seem like much.

The thought grew into an idea to start a vintage jewelry business—making jewelry from people's old treasures. A grandmother's brooch, a broken necklace, a lone earring from an heirloom set—each piece could be transformed into something a person could wear every day. It could become something they could celebrate and honor.

After releasing a very healthy and fully rehabilitated Squeeker into the wild, Bonnie started Squirrel Treasures Vintage Jewelry.

But that wasn't all the little squirrel did to change Bonnie's life.

After experiencing firsthand the joy of rescuing and caring for an animal in need, Bonnie decided to open a rescue farm so she could help other animals as well.

Piccolo Farms Animal Sanctuary is located in Whites Creek, Tennessee, a safe place for a variety of animals—each one broken in some way but finding healing, hope, and a forever home.

PAWS & PONDER . . .

What things do you treasure? If you could fill your house with anything, what would it be? How does wisdom build a house? In what ways do wisdom and knowledge help you fill your home and heart with lasting treasures?

Paws & Pray

Father, help me to build my home and life on the wisdom that comes from you. There are so many things competing for my attention—competing to be treasures in my heart. Give me discernment to know which treasures to pursue and which to relinquish. And stir my heart to treasure you most of all.

5 5

℘A GOOD ℬOY

A person may think their own ways are right,

but the LORD weighs the heart.

PROVERBS 21:2, NIV

BUFF WAS READY. The air was charged with excitement, and the walls of the training facility reverberated with the sounds of eager dogs.

Gary, Buff's owner, took it all in. This was the moment they had been training for—the culmination of countless hours working with his cocker spaniel.

From the day he got Buff, Gary recognized that the puppy had an innate intelligence and willingness to please. Buff flew through puppy obedience classes, the requirements to become a Canine Good Citizen, and other training sessions. Buff proved to be a star student, quickly rising to the top of each and every class he participated in.

Gary was encouraged by the obedience school owner to enter Buff in an AKC obedience competition. He worked with Buff every day, going through the routine and commands until they were second nature to the dog.

When the day of the competition finally arrived, Gary knew his dog was ready. And after watching several of the other contestants, he also knew his dog could win.

Buff executed each command flawlessly, eager to receive the next one from Gary.

More and more dogs were being disqualified. Yet Buff kept moving higher and higher up the leader board. Finally, he was at the top.

There was only one more event to go for Buff to be crowned the overall winner.

It had been a long day, and Gary suppressed a yawn as the judges set up for the final event—a test of the dog's ability to hold a sit-stay while the trainer leaves the room for two minutes.

Gary looked down at Buff, who was resting at his feet. Apparently, Gary was not the only one feeling the effects of the late hour.

After a short respite, Gary and Buff were called to the judging area.

He patted Buff on the back. "You've got this, boy. Just do it the way you've done it every other time, and you'll take home the trophy."

The dog glanced at Gary, then fixed his gaze straight ahead. He was ready.

Gary got Buff into position and commanded him to sit. Making sure Buff's attention was focused on his hand, Gary gave the signal for the stay command. Then he exited through a door where he would remain out of Buff's sight for two minutes.

The crowd seemed to hold their breath as Buff sat perfectly still, awaiting Gary's return.

Buff's eyes were fixed on the door.

One minute passed.

Buff sat like a statue.

One minute thirty seconds passed.

Buff hadn't moved.

One minute forty seconds passed.

Buff let out a sigh of exhaustion, then slowly dropped into a down-stay. His eyes were still fixed on the door.

When Buff moved from a sit-stay into a down-stay, he was instantly disqualified.

Gary opened the door.

Immediately, Buff sat up straight, tail wagging. In his mind he had stayed, and he was obviously proud of himself.

When Gary gave him the come command, Buff took off like a shot toward Gary, proud as a peacock. He practically slid past his owner as he came to a stop. In that moment, the world according to Buff was great.

Gary smiled and patted Buff's head, then dropped to one knee and hugged him.

"You're a good boy," he said, meaning the words with all his heart. "And you did a good job. A very good job."

Buff received a green honorable mention ribbon, not a trophy, that day. The two of them never competed again. Gary enjoyed training with Buff, but he realized that no numerical score could ever fully measure one's worth or abilities.

And sometimes, we all need a moment to lie down and take a little rest.

PAWS & PONDER...

Were you surprised by Gary's encouraging words to Buff? How did his words make you feel? Today's proverb says that God weighs our hearts; another translation uses the phrase "he examines our hearts." If Gary had been able to examine Buff's heart that night, what would he have found? If God were to examine your heart right now, what would he find? A heart actively seeking to know him and follow him? Or a heart trying to go its own way? Take a few minutes and ask God to examine your heart and your motives. Then spend some time confessing and reflecting on what he reveals.

Paws & Pray

Lord, examine my heart and my motives. Reveal any willful sins I am harboring, as well as any sins I have unknowingly allowed to grow. Forgive me, Lord, and give me a clean heart. I love you and want to obey you.

5 6

₰OSIE'S ₰CAR

Wounds from a friend can be trusted, but an enemy multiplies kisses.

PROVERBS 27:6, NIV

ROSIE, THE EIGHTY-POUND Golden retriever, lay trembling under the bench seat in one of the veterinary clinic's exam rooms, her body pressed against the back wall. The cream-colored tile floor would have provided the perfect camouflage if not for the fluffy tail draped across Jordan's feet. The moment Dr. Burroughs opened the door, Rosie tucked her tail around herself and whimpered.

"Well, clearly she has forgiven and forgotten," Dr. Burroughs said, laughing and lowering herself to the floor to pat the dog's back end.

Rosie had never been a fan of the vet—often whining and shaking during her appointments—but an emergency surgical procedure six days ago to treat a large ruptured cyst had taken her fear of the vet to an entirely new level. Jordan had worried she wouldn't be able to get her dog inside the animal clinic for her appointment that morning.

Thankfully, Rosie's love of treats kept her moving from the car to the lobby of the clinic, as Rosie nuzzled the morsels cupped in Jordan's hand. But once they stepped inside the exam room, Rosie's treat obsession stopped, and she began to cower and shake.

After leading the nervous dog away from the wall, Dr. Burroughs examined the six-inch scar on her right shoulder.

"It's looking really good," she said. "There are no signs of infection. I'm so glad we saw her when we did, or things could have gotten much worse."

Jordan cringed at the thought. She placed her hand on Rosie's head, rubbing her thumb gently against the Golden's soft ear. *Thank you, Lord,* she silently prayed.

"As the incision continues to heal," Dr. Burroughs said, "it will likely get very itchy. If Rosie starts scratching, try putting her in a T-shirt. That should discourage her. Also, she's getting a blister from licking the IV site. Let's put her head in a cone for a few days. Do you have one at home?"

Jordan nodded. "We still have the one you gave us when she was spayed."

With a few final parting instructions, Rosie bolted down the hall, paused just long enough for Jordan to pay the bill, and then dragged her human to the car.

For days, Rosie stared forlornly at Jordan, pleading with her to remove the cone of shame and the coordinating T-shirt of humiliation. Jordan didn't know whether to laugh or cry at the pitiful sight. Rosie had been a trouper about all the post-surgery paraphernalia, but it was evident the dog wanted a break from the cumbersome cone.

"I know it's been hard, Rosie," Jordan sympathized, running her fingers through Rosie's thick fur at the base of the cone. "I wish I could make you understand that this is all for your good. It stinks now, but when it's over, you are going to be better and healthier and stronger, okay?"

Jordan's inspiring pep talk did little to lift Rosie's spirits.

"All right, girl," Jordan said, sitting down, surrendering to her dog's silent pleas. "Maybe it is time for a little breather. What do you think?"

Jordan pulled the velcro tabs apart, and the cone dropped to the floor. She pulled the T-shirt over Rosie's head. After one mighty shake, Rosie slid onto Jordan's lap. The dog made a litany of grateful sounds as she celebrated her temporary freedom. Jordan gingerly ran her finger-tips over the peach fuzz fur growing over the incision. The new fur was already camouflaging the scar.

Rosie would never understand the reason behind the wound or the scar, but Jordan did. And Rosie trusted Jordan.

Trust. It made everything—even the annoying cone—tolerable for the dog that had fallen asleep on Jordan's lap.

PAWS & PONDER...

What does Proverbs 27:6 mean to you? Why can you trust wounds from a friend? How do those wounds differ from others you might experience? How can you tell the difference between a healing wound and a harmful wound? What do you learn about God's heart through Rosie's story?

Paws & Pray

Lord, wounds are not pleasant. And yet you tell us in your Word that the wounds of a friend can be trusted. God, you are the best friend I will ever know. Deepen my trust in you and help me understand that the wounds you allow are for a greater purpose, even if I don't grasp that purpose this side of eternity. Please strengthen me as I wait for you to heal me wherever I am hurting.

57

⟨B⟩LIND ⟨F⟩AITH

It is foolish to follow your own opinions. Be safe,

and follow the teachings of wiser people.

PROVERBS 28:26, GNT

SUNLIGHT GLINTED off the shallow lake as children darted in and out of the water. Relieved parents sat in camping chairs along the water's edge—basking in the first rain-free day of the week. Squirrels scampered about in search of fallen acorns. Hikers enjoyed the trails while kayakers found new places along the river to explore. And dogs, with their noses to the damp ground, followed new scents, trying to hurry their owners.

All except one.

"Mama, that dog doesn't have any eyes," a little girl said, loud enough to get everyone's attention around them.

Her mother shushed her, but the little girl's curiosity wasn't satisfied. With her blonde head cocked to the side, she watched the dog walk off leash beside his owner. The dog looked just like Winston, her grandparents' dog. But instead of big brown eyes, this dog only had slits where his eyes should have been.

Across the lake from the blind dog, three big dogs were barking and chasing tennis balls thrown into the water.

"Moe, listen," the lady said to the sightless dog before throwing a tennis ball into the water.

Ploop.

Moe's ears perked as his head tilted to the right. His nostrils twitched and his mouth opened slightly.

"Moe," the woman spoke softly. "Get your ball."

The young observer held her breath as the blind dog ran into the water after his ball. She moved closer for a better view. *How would a blind dog ever find a ball in the water?*

Moe made a beeline straight to it. With the ball securely in his mouth, Moe proudly brought it back to his owner.

"Good boy, Moe," she said, patting his wet fur. "Good get."

The little girl wondered how he lost his eyes. She wondered if it had hurt. Or if he was born like that. She squeezed her own eyes shut—wanting to experience what Moe was experiencing.

As Moe dropped his ball at his owner's feet and walked back to the water's edge, a group of small children came running toward the lake with buckets and shovels swinging.

"Moe, come. Side," the little girl heard the woman tell her dog.

Moe walked straight to her and pressed his left side against her legs.

"Good, Moe," she said, handing the dog a treat. "Okay, let's walk."

Moe heeled in step with his owner—not distracted like many dogs, but straight and purposeful, and completely in tune with the person who loved him so much.

PAWS & PONDER...

Amid all the distraction and noise at the lake, Moe had to listen carefully to the voice of his owner. Are you listening closely to God's voice today? Are you trusting him to lead and direct your steps? What problem are you facing today that you need to drop at the Lord's feet?

Paws & Pray

Lord, I am so prone to zigzag through this life—going my own way, getting distracted, pursuing foolish things. Father, please quiet my heart today. Let me sit silently before you and simply listen. I long to hear your voice. Direct my steps and lead me on the path that honors you.

58

AN ADVENTURE FOR MOXIE

A cheerful heart is good medicine,

but a crushed spirit dries up the bones.

PROVERBS 17:22, NIV

"I'M AFRAID IT'S NOT GREAT NEWS," the veterinarian said to Ken and Janet, giving their cat, Moxie, a sympathetic ear rub. "The tests confirm a significant heart defect."

After discussing the pros and cons of a complex surgery and experimental medications for Moxie, the vet looked apologetically at the recently retired couple. "Why don't you take a few days to think things over and we can talk next week."

It didn't take Ken and Janet long to reach a decision about the little tan and white cat who had mysteriously appeared in their barn a month earlier. They would let him enjoy whatever time he had left without putting him through the ordeal of surgery or side effects from strong medications.

Two days after letting the vet know their decision, Ken presented Janet with an idea. "What would you say to giving Moxie a grand adventure and making every day count for him?"

"You mean you want to take him with us on the boat?" Janet asked in amused disbelief. "The boat we are going to live on for the next several years?"

"Well . . . why not?" Ken said with a chuckle, excitement brimming in his eyes. "I mean, how many cats can say they've circumnavigated the world?"

Janet agreed.

The next few months were full of final preparations—the culmination of five years of planning. They sold their house, stocked up on provisions and equipment, said their goodbyes to friends and family, and then finally stepped aboard the *Aquila*, their fifty-two-foot Santa Cruz sailboat—with Moxie in tow.

After exploring every inch of the performance cruiser's hull and cabin, Moxie pawed at the rigging, sashayed across seats, and then lay regally in the bow.

"I think he approves," Ken said, motoring out of the marina to begin their grand adventure.

The first few days were rough for Moxie as he struggled to adjust to life on the water. When the sea got choppy, he refused to eat or use the litter box. He crammed his body into the small, round stainless steel sink in the aft head whenever the winds picked up. And Moxie left quite a few messes to clean up in the middle of the night when he would sneak out of his sleeping quarters to "play" with the squid that had the misfortune of landing on the deck. But eventually the cat and the humans settled into a routine.

As the days turned into weeks, and months, and years, Moxie experienced moments many humans have never witnessed: fishing from a dinghy in the middle of the Caribbean, watching an annual canoe race in Tahiti, enduring a lengthy quarantine in New Zealand, playing with dolphins off the coast of Tasmania, watching sea turtles swim in Fiji, and surviving a harrowing storm in Australia.

During their time at sea, Moxie became well known by the sailing community—a small group of fellow circumnavigators who traveled within a few hundred miles of each other. At least once a week the floating community would anchor their large vessels and congregate in their dinghies, tying them together while they watched the sun sink into the sea. Moxie—who often attended the sunset soirees—would jump from dinghy to dinghy, greeting the people and accepting tidbits and treats.

"That is one happy cat," Ken would often hear people remark about their feline companion. It always made him smile. For the fact was, no one knew how long Moxie had to live, but the cat embraced each moment as its own great adventure. And in the process he inspired a small fleet of others to do the same.

PAWS & PONDER . . .

Do you share Moxie's view of life that each day is a great adventure? Or does each day feel like a struggle you simply must endure? How would you describe your heart and spirit? Tell God how you honestly feel and ask him to breathe life and adventure back into your spirit.

Paws & Pray

Lord, my spirit can feel crushed under the weight of daily responsibilities, hurts, and fears. And yet I know this is not how you want me to live. You invite me to give you my burdens and walk in your strength. Father, lighten my heart right now. Remind me who you are and who I am to you. I want to experience the grand adventure you have in store for me.

The righteous choose their friends carefully.

PROVERBS 12:26, NIV

59

SUNNY'S HEDGEHOG

A peaceful heart leads to a healthy body;
jealousy is like cancer in the bones.

PROVERBS 14:30

SUNNY HAD BEEN THE BABY of the family for four years. Darrell and Jen had adopted the reddish-blonde Golden retriever on their one-year anniversary, and since that time Sunny had enjoyed her only-child status. She accompanied them on road trips, was allowed on the furniture, and even was included in the family portrait.

Sunny reveled in the attention and was often teased by Jen and Darrell's friends and family for being a bit of a princess.

However, her diva-like status was about to take a major hit.

The first clue was when Darrell and Jen left for several days without her. This had never happened before. Sunny liked her petsitter well enough, but she wanted her people back.

On a cold January morning, Darrell and Jen came home. When the front door opened, Sunny greeted Darrell with a welcome-home jump.

But before Sunny could greet Jen with an equally joyful jump, Darrell pulled her back by the collar and held her.

"Gentle, girl," he commanded.

Sunny's nostrils began to quiver, and she raised her nose to take in a new scent. She looked as though she were asking, *What is that? What is Jen carrying?*

Then a strange cry filled the room.

Jen sat down on the sofa, holding a squirmy bundle in her arms. She nodded at Darrell.

Darrell got a firmer grip on Sunny's collar and led the dog to the sofa.

Sunny wanted to jump up, but Darrell kept her in check. She sat in front of Jen and watched as Jen pulled the blanket back, revealing the tiniest human Sunny had ever seen.

Desperate to smell this newcomer, Sunny inched closer and closer. When she tried to lick the fidgety baby, Darrell pulled her back.

All day Sunny stayed close to Jen and the little person they called Andrew.

The next day, Sunny anxiously awaited her morning walk. But it never came. Darrell and Jen seemed more tired than usual. Sunny suspected the tiny human had something to do with their exhaustion.

Two days later, Sunny stood by the back door hoping to go for a ride in the car.

But Darrell and Jen never left the house. Instead, Jen's parents brought over some tasty looking things called diapers. Sunny didn't know what they were, but she made it her mission to try to grab as many as she could—some tasted better than others.

Day after day, Sunny waited for her life to get back to normal.

But each day Jen and Darrell seemed busy with the baby. Holding him, feeding him, washing him, and talking to him.

Even though she was doing more observing than interacting, Sunny liked the little person. She felt a strong desire to guard and protect him, but she also missed being the focus of Darrell and Jen's attention.

Days passed. Sunny decided to take a different approach.

Jen was sitting on the sofa holding the baby, so Sunny walked over to her toy bin and picked up her large stuffed hedgehog. It wasn't quite as big as the baby, but it was close. She took her hedgehog over to the sofa and lay down with it nestled between her front paws.

Later, when Jen went into the nursery to feed the baby, Sunny lay down at Jen's feet and positioned her hedgehog against her belly.

And that night when Darrell and Jen put the baby in a large dish inside of the big scary bathtub and began to wash him, Sunny dropped her hedgehog into the bathtub for a bath too.

For two whole weeks, everything Jen did with the baby Sunny mimicked with her hedgehog.

Darrell and Jen laughed and smiled a lot at Sunny—although Sunny didn't know why.

Then about a month after the baby's arrival, Darrell asked Sunny if she wanted to go for a ride. Sunny jumped out of her bed and ran to the door—leaving her hedgehog behind.

After that day, Sunny didn't play as much with her hedgehog. She didn't seem to need it anymore.

Her life wasn't like it was before, but it was okay. Now she had three family members to love.

Sunny suspected that by the way the baby was growing, someday he might be big enough to play with her. She was certain Andrew would be even more fun than her hedgehog.

PAWS & PONDER...

In what areas do you struggle most with jealousy? Do you long for peace and contentment in those areas? What are some differences between a peace-filled heart and a heart full of jealousy?

Paws & Pray

Lord, let me be someone who is marked by peace and contentment. Forgive me for being consumed by jealousy and envy. Father, I confess those feelings to you now and ask you to replace them with gratitude for what you've given me. Help me to embrace your perfect will for my life and release my insecurities to you.

60

SAVING RILEY

Do not withhold good from those who deserve it
when it's in your power to help them.

PROVERBS 3:27

"BAILEY MUST BE THE WORLD'S most tolerant dog," Nancy said, as she watched their new puppy chew the yellow Lab's tail.

It was Christmas Eve and her husband, Wayne, had come home from the animal shelter—with a puppy.

"I thought Sherie could use a dog of her own," Wayne said in his defense when Nancy gave him *the look.*

"Clearly that dog," he said, pointing to Bailey at Nancy's feet, "has eyes only for you. Our little girl needs a dog who will be devoted to her. And besides it's Christmas, and this little one needs a home. The poor thing barely survived being shot by her previous owner."

Nancy gasped. "What? How could . . . ? Oh my." She cradled the puppy's sandy white head.

Her husband handed the terrier-hound mix puppy to Nancy. "The shelter staff says she's fine now, although she still has the bullet lodged in her hip. It was too dangerous to take it out. It may give her problems in the future, but I just had—"

"To take her," Nancy finished. "Of course, you did. And I'm glad you did. Does she have a name?"

"The folks at the shelter called her Riley, but we can change it if you want."

Nancy studied the fidgety puppy. "Riley's perfect."

For the first five minutes she was perfect. But as soon as Riley met Bailey, the newcomer turned into her version of the Looney Tunes Tasmanian devil. She bit at Bailey's ankles. She nibbled at her ears. Then she ran circles around Bailey before ricocheting against the bigger dog.

Yet Bailey never lashed out at her. Maybe she was paralyzed with fear. Maybe she hoped if she remained still Riley would grow tired of the game and leave. Or maybe she was just trying to figure out why this little dog was going crazy.

Whatever the reason, Bailey permitted Riley to invade her personal space without retaliation.

"I'm sure Riley will calm down in a day or two," her husband stated confidently.

She did not.

In fact, over the next few weeks the puppy became even more feisty and spirited. When she was not using Bailey as a play gym, she was destroying the older dog's toys, trying to steal her food, and sneaking into her bed.

"She's had a rough start to her life," Nancy would explain to Bailey—more to remind herself. "We need to be patient with her."

Some days were harder than others. Especially the days the ankle-biting puppy chased poor Bailey round and round the pool deck. Their normally peaceful Florida backyard oasis had turned into a dog derby track.

A month after Riley joined their family, Nancy awoke before dawn, determined to get their lives back to normal. After feeding the dogs—and shooing Riley away from Bailey's breakfast—she let them outside to do their business. During the few moments of peace, Nancy searched on her laptop for dog trainers.

As she scrolled through the search results, she heard Bailey bark at the back door.

She opened the door to let her in, but her yellow Lab remained motionless and barked again.

"Bailey, come in," Nancy commanded.

Bailey barked again, took two steps back, and looked over her shoulder. A cold wind blew in the backdoor.

"Bailey, it's freezing; get in here. Riley, come!"

No Riley. Bailey moved back several more steps, again glancing toward the backyard.

A sense of dread radiated down Nancy's spine.

"Bailey, where's Riley?" Nancy couldn't keep the panic out of her voice.

The sixty-pound dog jumped as though she were bucking an imaginary rider and then ran to the pool deck. Nancy followed Bailey, trying to force her eyes to adjust to the predawn darkness.

She scanned the yard, she looked in the pool, and then she heard a faint whimper.

Riley had fallen in the spa tub. Only her black nose was visible above the water line. She was frantically clawing the water but could not reach the side. Nancy grabbed the puppy from the tub, ran her inside, and wrapped her in towels.

After warming up, Riley was fine.

"You are quite the hero, Bailey," Nancy praised the dog lying at her feet. "Even though this little one can make your life quite miserable, you still protected her. You are such a good dog."

Bailey lifted an eyebrow as Nancy carefully set Riley down beside her. And for the first time since joining their family, Riley lay down beside Bailey and fell fast asleep.

Nancy smiled at the two of them. She grabbed her phone and took a picture of the idyllic moment.

"Gotta have evidence. 'Cause heaven only knows how long this will last."

PAWS & PONDER...

Bailey was good to Riley, in spite of the frustration she experienced from the pesky little dog. Have you ever done something good to someone who did not deserve it? Has someone ever done the same for you when you did not deserve it? Think of someone you can surprise today with an act of kindness.

Paws & Pray

Lord, thank you for being good to me when I do not deserve it. Please help me to have eyes to see others' needs and a heart and hands willing to respond to those needs. So many people around me are hurting, lost, lonely, and scared. Show me how I can look past my own circumstances today and see opportunities to help others, including those that drive me a bit crazy.

61

RUDY, SHAKE

Too much honey is bad for you,
and so is trying to win too much praise.

PROVERBS 25:27, GNT

"MAKE A WISH, LIAM," Andrea said, holding her son's Paw Patrol–themed cake. "And then you can blow out your candles."

Her little boy's face beamed with joy as he huffed and puffed, blowing out each candle one at a time.

"I'm four, Mama!" he said proudly, holding up three fingers.

Setting the cake down, Andrea kissed his head and showed him how to hold up four fingers.

"I'm four!" he repeated, showing the proper number of fingers to his friends who had come to celebrate with him.

The group of ten, six boys and four girls, talked loudly, their mouths full of blue and white cake. The topic of conversation revolved around dogs, both fictional and real.

After each one declared their favorite Paw Patrol dog, they took turns talking about their own dogs, or lack thereof.

"I don't have a dog," Claire said, her bottom lip sticking out in a perfect pout.

"You can pet Rudy," Liam said, pointing to his dog who sat in rapt attention beside him. Rudy was eyeing every bite of cake Liam put in his mouth.

As Andrea walked into the kitchen to put away the trays of chicken nuggets and fruit, she heard Liam add, "Rudy can do lots of tricks. Watch. Rudy, shake!"

Cheering erupted from the dining room.

"Rudy is in doggie heaven," she chuckled, knowing how much their pound pup adored attention.

Ever since they had brought him home from the SPCA, he had lived for their praise. If you weren't paying attention to the forty-pound dog, he would paw, jump, or bark to get you focused on him. It was both endearing and annoying—especially when Liam was napping.

"Rudy, shake!" another little voice commanded.

"Shake me, Rudy!" came another.

A round of giggles and squeals were followed by more commands to shake, sit, lie down, and dance!

Andrea laughed.

"I'm not sure Rudy knows the dance command, guys," she said, walking back into the dining room.

She came to an abrupt halt. Rudy's face, whiskers, nose, the tips of his ears, and his foot were decorated with blue splotches. *Is Rudy morphing into a Smurf?* Andrea wondered. The answer quickly became apparent as she watched a little hand reach down to shake Rudy's paw, before rewarding the dog with a piece of cake.

A reward Rudy was ecstatic to receive over and over again.

"Oh, Rudy," Andrea said with a sigh. "What a mess you are. And how sick you are surely going to be. It's time for you to leave the party."

Rudy was less than pleased when Andrea escorted him out of the room.

Of course, later than evening, Andrea was less than pleased to have to clean up the aftereffects of Rudy's impromptu trick demonstration.

"You just couldn't say no to the attention . . . or the cake, could ya, boy?"

PAWS & PONDER...

Too much of a good thing. How can trying to earn too much praise be bad for you? What do you risk when you allow the praise and attention of others to become the driving force of your life? Is there an area in your life right now where you are trying to please others more than God? Would you take a moment to confess that to the Lord?

Paws & Pray

Lord, how easy it is to seek the praise and attention of others above all else, even making myself sick in the process. Forgive me for being more concerned with what others say about me than with what you say about me. Help me to be content with who I am in you.

62

ΤHE ƐCLIPSE

The prudent see danger and take refuge,

but the simple keep going and pay the penalty.

PROVERBS 22:3, NIV

IT WAS NIGHTTIME AND JADE, a six-year-old shepherd mix, was on duty, sitting on the family's deck in the moonlight. Her ears were like two sonar devices, scanning the area for the slightest hint of a sound. The lovable and protective dog made it her responsibility to keep her family's two-acre property free from any and all wildlife. And she did her job well, often running off a deer heading toward the garden or a squirrel trying to make its way up the bird feeder. In the two years since Jade had been with her human family, she had yet to meet an animal she wouldn't chase.

As Jade kept watch, the family prepared for an impending celestial show—a lunar eclipse. Dave, his wife, Jill, and their two children, Alex and Emma, spread an old king-sized comforter on the deck. The air was bitterly cold, but Jill made sure they had plenty of fleece blankets and winter accessories to keep everyone warm.

"What is this thing called again?" Jill asked her science-obsessed son.

With a playful roll of his eyes, her teenager answered, "A super blood wolf moon total eclipse."

"That's just too many words for me to remember," Jill joked.

Dave dumped the pile of blankets in the middle of the comforter and the family quickly wrapped themselves up in fleece cocoons for the heavenly spectacle.

Jade was torn between keeping her post near the steps and being close to her family. She finally succumbed to their excitement and wedged herself between Alex and Emma. Laying her head on Emma's lap, the dog closed her eyes—oblivious to the awe-inspiring scene taking place above her head. The earth's shadow moved across the moon, swallowing it whole and changing it from white to charcoal to fiery red.

"This is so cool," Emma whispered. "The moon looks like a bouncy ball floating in the sky."

All of creation seemed to be still as the moon turned an even deeper shade of red.

But then an eerie howl broke the reverent silence, and Jade sprang to her feet. Jill's heart skipped a beat. Coyotes.

What would happen if Jade confronted a coyote?

Jill and Dave got up to stop Jade from charging into the pitch-black yard.

Yet the dog was not charging. She hadn't even left the deck. In fact, the normally headstrong, charge-first-ask-questions-later dog was standing quietly at the railing of the deck, her nose pressed between the slats, the hair at the nape of her neck standing straight up.

"Mama?" Emma whispered. "What made that howl?"

As soon as Jill said *coyote*, a second howl—this one much closer—pierced the night. Jade gave a quiet whine before circling her family and walking straight to the back door.

Jade sensed danger and instead of running at it, she was choosing to get away as fast as possible. And she was taking her family with her.

"Good girl, Jade!" Dave praised her when the family was safely inside. "What a smart dog you are!"

As the family rewarded Jade with treats and belly rubs, Jill smiled. The super blood wolf moon total eclipse had just been eclipsed by the heroic canine lying in the middle of her kitchen.

PAWS & PONDER...

What could have happened if Jade had run after the coyote? Not all dangers are as obvious as a howling coyote, so how can you recognize impending danger? Think of a potentially dangerous situation you are facing today. How might you seek refuge from that situation? What might happen if you don't?

Paws & Pray

Lord, help me stay close to you and to your Word so that I might recognize danger whenever it is near. You give me strength and I know I can run to you for refuge whenever I am afraid. Remind me of this truth when danger and temptation come my way.

63

WHAT A FRIEND

Love prospers when a fault is forgiven,
but dwelling on it separates close friends.

PROVERBS 17:9

"READY TO GO VISIT?" Sandee asked Tesla.

Her two-year-old Golden retriever looked intently at her. A wagging tail, raised ears, and open mouth indicated Tesla was definitely ready. In fact, the more time Sandee spent with her sweet-natured dog, the more she believed Tesla had actually been *born* ready to work as a therapy dog. Even as a young puppy, the sandy-colored Golden had been unusually calm and even-tempered, crucial traits for a therapy dog.

Especially one like Tesla, who worked with advanced-stage Alzheimer's patients.

Sandee led her dog into the multipurpose room, where a handful of residents were assembled. A couple sat together at a table, two women slumped down in their wheelchairs, and a man stood holding tightly to a walker. A few sets of eyes, bright with awareness, lit up as Tesla walked into the room.

She happily went to the outstretched hands beckoning her to come. If someone did not reach for her, Tesla would look at Sandee for guidance.

"Is it okay if my dog says hello to you?" Sandee would ask the resident. Rarely did anyone say no. And the moment they said yes, Tesla was at their side.

A bright-eyed woman at the table patted her knees and called, "Good doggie-doggie." Tesla responded immediately. The woman smiled wide as she stroked Tesla's long coat and giggled when Tesla gave her a paw to shake.

But then without any warning, the woman smacked Tesla on the nose and started screaming, "You're being so mean to me! You're a bad dog!"

Tesla cast a quick glance at Sandee—seeking instruction or reassurance. Quick to give both, Sandee knelt before her dog, rubbed her chest, told her she was a good girl, and then instructed her to stay by her side as the nursing staff gently led the weeping woman back to her room. Sandee offered a silent prayer for the woman, whose disease was clearly at an advanced stage.

Although Sandee was a little shaken, Tesla went right back to work, happily visiting every patient who beckoned her.

Week after week, Sandee and Tesla returned to the Alzheimer's care floor, and week after week, Sandee watched her dog lavish everyone with affection, attention, and companionship. The incident with the confused woman had not fazed Tesla at all. The dog held no grudge. And she wasn't the least bit wary of the other residents.

Several weeks later Sandee and Tesla were introduced to Maggie, a petite woman who had moved in just two days before. The director said that Maggie had neither spoken nor eaten since arriving. Sandee greeted Maggie, inviting her to pet Tesla.

The woman shook her head no.

Sandee smiled at the woman and then followed Tesla around the large room as she said hello to the other residents. After several minutes, Tesla made her way back to Maggie and sat quietly at her feet. At first Maggie seemed oblivious to the dog, whose front left paw rested against her foot. Over the next several minutes, Sandee watched as Maggie put her hand down and touched Tesla's head. Then Maggie leaned over and kissed Tesla. Sandee fought back tears as Maggie began talking to Tesla—telling the dog about a pink dress she sewed for the big dance and how pretty Tesla would look in a pink collar.

Maggie's entire countenance had changed. Her eyes looked brighter, her head was up, and much to Sandee's surprise and delight, Maggie began to sing. The sounds of hymns from long ago filled the multipurpose room, as one by one more and more voices joined in—including Sandee's, whose voice quavered with emotion.

As she sang the chorus to "What a Friend We Have in Jesus," she couldn't help but stare at her dog. Her precious canine girl whose willingness to overlook an offense and meet people where they were had led to a powerful and sacred moment.

PAWS & PONDER...

What blessings might have been missed had Tesla allowed one negative experience to affect her treatment of the nursing care residents? Have you ever allowed one bad experience to keep you from possible blessings? What role does discernment play in forgiveness and reconciliation?

Paws & Pray

Father, oftentimes it is much easier for me to hold on to a grudge than it is to release it and forgive. You want me to forgive others, just as you have forgiven me. I cannot do this without you. Lord, make me willing to forgive those who have wronged me, and give me insight to understand their actions and discernment to know how to move forward. I know you will help me with each and every step.

Do not plot harm against your neighbor,
who lives trustfully near you.

PROVERBS 3:29, NIV

64

STEPPING OUT FOR CHARLIE

The very steps we take come from God; otherwise

how would we know where we're going?

PROVERBS 20:24, MSG

MARIE'S STEPS WERE HESITANT as she walked toward the animal rescue shelter. She couldn't even remember the last time she walked with confidence.

Actually, she could.

The last time she walked with the assurance of a life going according to plan would have been before her husband's cancer diagnosis.

Before their world was turned upside down and she lost the love of her life.

Ever since cancer entered the picture, Marie's steps had felt anything but confident. The curveball life had thrown her—leaving her alone for the first time in her life—had left her shaken and uncertain of every decision.

Even the decision to rescue a dog.

Marie was grateful for the companionship of her little cat, Cashmere, who had been a source of comfort after Marie's husband died, yet she was struggling with living in such a quiet house. There was no one at home to greet her when she walked in the door. Having had dogs off and on through most of her life, Marie decided it was time to get another dog.

However, as she stood outside the rescue shelter, she questioned her decision.

Am I really ready for a dog?

Can I take care of one by myself?

Will I be able to train it?

Doubts slowed her steps, but a determination she hadn't felt in a long time urged her to keep going.

In the shelter she saw a scrawny little Shih Tzu who lay shaking in a cage. The only information the shelter had on the dog was that he was about two years old. His past was a mystery. But Marie knew she wanted to give him a future.

Marie adopted the dog that day and named him Charlie. Poor Charlie shook during the entire drive home and seemed afraid of everything— even Marie. He was trembling in her arms as she carried him inside. *How will he react to Cashmere?*

To Marie's astonishment, the moment Cashmere approached Charlie, her nervous dog seemed to calm down. Cat and dog examined each other for several minutes, then as if an unspoken request had been made for a house tour, Cashmere led Charlie from the kitchen to the family room. Eventually the two lay down for the night, with Charlie snuggled up next to Cashmere.

Marie was grateful for the bond between the two animals, especially with Charlie's intense anxiety. He eventually grew less fearful around her but was terrified of everyone else—especially men.

This became clear their first night at obedience school when Charlie spent most of the class hiding under Marie's chair. When a man approached Charlie, trying to coax him to come out, the Shih Tzu was so frightened that he soaked the floor underneath him.

Over time, with gentle encouragement and consistent training, Charlie became more social and secure. Marie was happy that Charlie had stopped hiding and shaking when her grandchildren visited. Now he seemed to love their attention. Marie was even able to start taking Charlie for walks without him trembling or crying.

Charlie still struggled with certain fears, especially fireworks, thunderstorms, large dogs, and noisy trucks, but Marie was so proud of how far he had come.

Actually, both of us have come a long way, Marie often thought when she and Charlie were on their evening walk or when she took Charlie with her to the Bible study she co-led at an assisted living facility.

Marie's steps were no longer hesitant and uncertain. Though her life did not turn out the way she had hoped, God used a little rescue dog to remind her that she was safe with him. Even when her steps of faith felt a little bit shaky, he had promised to always be there with her—to steady her, to guide her way, and to be her source of strength and hope.

PAWS & PONDER...

Has life thrown you a curveball you didn't see coming? Do your steps feel hesitant and unsure? Where will your help come from today? Who guards your steps? Will you trust the Maker of heaven and earth to steady and guide you today?

Paws & Pray

Lord God, you are the Maker of heaven and earth. My help and my hope come from you. Father, guide me today and keep me from faltering. When I become fearful, remind me that you are beside me. Increase my trust in you; I want to become closer to you.

65

SIR BUBBLES

Your will to live can sustain you when you are sick,

but if you lose it, your last hope is gone.

PROVERBS 18:14, GNT

"SIR BUBBLES IS BELLY UP," Brian whispered to his wife, Shelby, as he entered the kitchen.

"What!" she quietly squealed, casting a quick look at their seven-year-old son, Ryker. "He can't be dead already!"

Sir Bubbles the goldfish was a recent addition to the family—Ryker's prize for winning a game of ring toss at the fair. Brian tried not to dwell on how many goldfish he could have bought at a pet store for the amount of money he spent on the nine rounds of ring toss. But seeing the joy on Ryker's face after winning the fish made the price not quite as painful.

And there was no denying how much Ryker loved the little orange and white fish.

Ryker had set the tank on his bedside table so he could watch Sir Bubbles at night. He read books to him at bedtime and included Sir Bubbles in his nightly prayers.

Three days after Sir Bubbles's arrival, Ryker announced that Sir Bubbles was the world's greatest fish and his bestest friend ever.

So when Brian discovered Sir Bubbles floating at the top of the tank one morning, just a week after Ryker's declaration of friendship, he ran down the stairs prepared to console his son.

But Ryker had been oblivious to the fact that his scaly friend had expired.

After informing Shelby of the news, Brian turned to their son.

"Hey, buddy," he said with a gentle smile. "Did you see Sir Bubbles this morning?"

"Yep," Ryker answered, his eyes never leaving his cartoon playing on the TV. "He was sleepin'. So I came downstairs real quiet so I didn't wake him up."

"Oh. Right . . . yeah . . . well," Brian stammered, looking at Shelby for help.

Ryker cut him off. "Daddy, can we talk later? I gotta finish my show before Anderson's party."

"Oh, right, you're going to Anderson's birthday party today," Brian mumbled as he led Shelby by the arm into their downstairs office.

"I can't tell him," Brian blurted out. "He's so happy. I can't tell him his bestest little fish buddy is dead."

Shelby gave him *the* look.

"We have to tell him," she said. "But we can wait till after the party."

Thirty minutes later Shelby and Ryker pulled out of the driveway to head to the party. Brian quickly followed—but to the pet store.

"I need a goldfish," Brian told the teenage girl stationed in the fish section at the pet store. He held his thumb and index finger several inches apart. "And it needs to be about this long."

"Okay," the girl said, taking a small square net and lowering it into a tank full of goldfish.

Sir Bubbles II was quickly bagged, paid for, and brought home. As Brian raced upstairs to switch the two goldfish, Shelby returned and found him in Ryker's room.

"Do you think we should flush the fish now or wait for . . . What is that?" she asked, pointing at the plastic bag in Brian's hand.

"Sir Bubbles," Brian stated matter-of-factly.

"Uh, no it's not," Shelby laughed. "Sir Bubbles is orange and white . . . and dead. That fish is all orange and very much not dead. Nice try!"

"I just didn't want Ryker to be upset."

Shelby hugged her husband, then laughed again at the pitiful Sir Bubbles impersonator.

"Well, I guess we'll just make the switch and see if he notices," she offered.

Brian took the tank into the bathroom to prepare Sir Bubbles for a burial at sea—or rather the sewer. He removed the lid of the tank and slipped his hand under Sir Bubbles's lifeless body.

He quickly jerked his hand out of the tank, water splashing all over the counter.

Sir Bubbles had twitched.

Sir Bubbles had quivered.

And then . . . Sir Bubbles swam.

Brian and Shelby stood dumbfounded, trying to make sense of the resurrected fish.

"You saw him floating in there, right?" Brian asked, feeling as though he had just witnessed Lazarus's emergence from the tomb. "I mean he was floating sideways. He was . . . dead. Right?"

Shelby inspected the lid of the tank. She pointed to the filter—the cover was missing.

"We must not have put the cover back on after cleaning it last night," she said, studying the now healthy-looking fish. "The poor thing must have swum too close. I wonder how long he was immobilized by the suction."

Brian was impressed. "Sir Bubs, you are one tough fish. But then again you have a lot to live for, don't ya? You have the love of an awesome kid who thinks you are the world's greatest fish."

Shelby cleared her throat and held up the plastic bag containing the Sir Bubbles replacement. "So, now that we have Sir Bubbles aka Sir Lazarus back, what, pray tell, are we going to do with this?"

Brian got a sheepish look. "Think Anderson wants a fish for his birthday?"

PAWS & PONDER ...

Brian wanted to protect his son from Sir Bubbles's "death." How have you tried to protect someone from heartache? What was the result? The story of Sir Bubbles had a happy ending, but unfortunately happy endings are never guaranteed in life. How can you still have hope in the midst of pain and loss? Who is the source of your help and hope?

Paws & Pray

Lord, you are my hope and my helper. When all else fails, you never will. Steady my heart today. Fix my eyes on you. Remind me that you—the almighty, all powerful, loving, holy, and just God—are my hope. Reinforce my faith in you every day.

66

$\mathcal{M}$ALACHI

Whoever heeds instruction is on the path to life,

but he who rejects reproof leads others astray.

PROVERBS 10:17, ESV

THE SIX-WEEK-OLD BLACK-AND-WHITE speckled puppy ran straight to Allison. He was the first of the energetic siblings to reach her. His exuberant greeting was all the confirmation Allison needed that he was meant to be hers.

"I've never seen him run to someone like that," said Colette, the puppies' foster caregiver. "It's like he knows you came for him."

Allison's heart swelled. She had indeed come for him.

And yet, up until a few days ago, she hadn't even thought about getting a dog. But the moment she had seen the puppy's face on her phone screen and learned that he needed a home, she couldn't get him out of her mind.

Am I letting my emotions get the best of me? she wondered.

However, the conviction only increased. Day after day, as she sat quietly before the Lord, she continued to hear him whisper to her soul that she and the puppy belonged together.

It didn't make any sense, and yet she knew she had to obey. She was already beginning to think of a name.

During her visit, Allison learned all she could about the puppy. She learned about his painful abandonment, his harrowing rescue by the Underdog Ranch Pet Adoption who swooped in and saved the litter from being euthanized, and she learned of his temperament—at least as much of it as Colette had been able to observe in the three weeks she had been fostering the puppies. Colette described the puppy as inquisitive yet reserved and guarded.

She's describing me, Allison thought.

As Allison held the soft ball of fur, she knew they were meant for each other. Looking in his eyes, she saw her own past reflected in their depths, and she prayed the puppy might see a glimpse of his future in hers.

Looking in his eyes was like looking in the eyes of a tiny little angel. Angel.

Malachi. Allison had been reading from the book of Malachi and knew the name meant both messenger and angel.

"Hi, Malachi," she whispered as she nuzzled the puppy. "That's a perfect name for you."

Four weeks later, Allison brought Malachi home.

It took a while for him to adjust, but eventually he began to settle into his life . . . just as Allison started to struggle in hers.

Years of repressed and undiagnosed anxiety started to bubble to the surface of Allison's consciousness, resulting in a barrage of symptoms— some quite intense.

It was during one such episode that Malachi stopped chewing on his toy and ran to Allison. He jumped on the sofa where she was lying and draped himself across her chest. After several minutes, Allison's heart rate slowed, her breathing steadied, and the episode passed. She hugged Malachi tightly, marveling at how perfectly his name fit him—he was, in fact, *her angel.*

Time and time again, little Malachi was there for Allison when her anxiety threatened to overwhelm her.

After seeking the counsel of trusted friends and professionals who helped her identify the source of her anxiety and begin to process through it, she shared how helpful Malachi was during her episodes.

As she talked, she felt God whisper to her soul, *"He was meant for you. Train him to be your service dog."*

Allison's jaw dropped. The puppy she hadn't been looking for, the anxiety she hadn't known was lurking—God was aware of everything and he had provided. He had asked her to say yes to his plan. To trust and obey.

Allison quickly got to work learning how to train and certify a service dog—*her* service dog.

Thankfully, Malachi proved to be a quick learner, easily mastering each new command. But being a young dog who was easily distracted, getting him to obey his commands outside of the house was more of a challenge.

Yet every day when Allison worked with Malachi, teaching him to listen to her voice, to watch her face, and to trust her instructions, she sensed God working in a similar way within her. She was being led to a deeper level of trust, healing, and faith in him.

It hasn't been easy, and just like Malachi, Allison has had to fight hard to stay focused on the voice and face of the one who loves her more than any other.

But she knows that it is worth it. Because every day as they are both being made new—redeemed and restored—they are able to help others find hope, healing, and new life.

PAWS & PONDER...

Allison heeded the instruction to get Malachi, even though at first she was hesitant to do so. Are you sometimes hesitant to heed God's instructions? Can you recall a time you heeded an instruction from the Lord? What was the result? Can you recall a time you dismissed his instruction? How did it turn out? Is there an instruction you need to act upon today?

Paws & Pray

God, you are my loving Father, and yet so often I am hesitant to trust and obey you when your Spirit convicts me. Forgive me for not heeding your instructions as I should. Lord, focus my heart and mind on your voice and your beautiful face, so that I too might find hope, healing, and life.

67

ṮHE ṮHREE ꞒANINE ẶMIGOS

Walk with the wise and become wise,

for a companion of fools suffers harm.

PROVERBS 13:20, NIV

CHIEF, A LITTLE YELLOW LAB PUPPY, cowered behind Bill in their backyard as two big dogs ran toward him. The owners were trying in vain to get their dogs under control.

"It's okay, Chief," Bill said calmly. "Those big crazy dogs are gonna be your best friends."

Chief poked his head between Bill's ankles. Clearly, the twelve-week-old pup had some reservations about these alleged "best buddies."

Sunny, a reddish-blonde two-year-old Golden belonging to Bill's daughter, Jen, and Samson, a year-old black Lab belonging to his sister Judy, were bounding up to Chief. The three sniffed one another from nose to tail and back again, as Bill hugged his daughter and sister.

It was a special day that had been long in the making.

Each of the dogs represented a new beginning for their owners.

To newly married Jen, Sunny symbolized the future and endless possibilities.

To Judy, whose dog Samson entered her life at the end of a painful season, her loyal companion represented hope and redemption.

And for Bill, who had recently lost both his best friend and his brother-in-law to cancer, his new puppy Chief represented new life.

Once the initial investigation was done, Sunny and Samson began chasing each other through the yard. Chief took a few hesitant steps away from Bill, looking back at his human and then at the fast-moving dogs.

"Go on, Chief," Bill encouraged the puppy. "Join the fun."

Chief went for it. His little legs pumped hard to keep up with Sunny and Samson. But after a few minutes, the three were romping happily together.

Eventually, Sunny grew tired of the chase game and went off to catch lizards—her favorite pastime. Chief watched Sunny intently as she hunted. After a few minutes, he began following along behind her as she stalked her prey. Bill laughed when Chief mimicked Sunny and pounced on a blade of grass after Sunny had pounced on an unsuspecting lizard.

Samson, who was not as enamored by lizards as Sunny, went off in search of his favorite toy—a tennis ball. When he found one, he ran over to Bill, dropped it at his feet, and dashed off in anticipation of the throw.

Samson's excitement caught Chief's attention, so he abandoned Sunny and the lizards and watched Samson catch several balls. Bill found a second ball and threw it a little closer for his puppy. Chief pounced on the ball as Sunny had pounced on her lizard and then ran it back to Bill and dropped it just as Samson had.

Eventually, the three dogs were hot and tired. After lapping up three bowls of water, they lay together in a cool, shaded area of the yard.

"It didn't take long for them to become the three amigos," Bill said.

Sunny, Samson, and Chief spent plenty of time together over the next eight years, and their owners enjoyed it as much as the canines.

Sunny, the gentle huntress who kept the boys in line.

Samson, the faithful friend who never grew tired of fetch.

And Chief, the loyal companion who brought joy to so many.

Three dogs who learned so much from one another. And who by modeling loyalty, friendship, persistence, and a joy for life, taught their humans even more.

PAWS & PONDER...

Why is it important to choose wise friends? What are some examples of harm or danger that might befall the "companion of fools"? If you are a parent, how can you help your children choose wise friends? What qualities mark a person as a wise friend?

Paws & Pray

Lord God, you are the source of all wisdom. Grant me good judgment when it comes to choosing friends. And help me to be a wise friend to others. When I take my lead from you, I know I will lead others well.

6 8

GOOD GIRL, GIDGET

Direct your children onto the right path,
and when they are older, they will not leave it.

PROVERBS 22:6

GIDGET, A THREE-YEAR-OLD Goldendoodle stood defiantly in the kitchen, trying to conceal the balled-up sock in her mouth. She eyed Kate, willfully disobeying the command she had just given.

"Gidget, come," Kate repeated.

Her dog turned and took a step in the opposite direction.

Gidget was the most strong-willed dog Kate had ever known. She also happened to be the smartest dog she had ever known—traits Kate was becoming convinced might be related.

Kate had enrolled Gidget in puppy obedience school and learned that the Goldendoodle definitely had a strong will, but she also had a strong desire for treats.

Whenever Gidget obeyed Kate's commands, she received a treat, followed by the words, "Good girl, Gidget!"

Gidget had grown into a wonderful dog who brought joy into Kate's life. And yet, Gidget's willfulness remained fully intact. Kate couldn't break her from stealing socks.

Whenever Gidget snatched a sock, the commands she knew quite well, such as "drop it" and "come," were ignored.

However, recently Kate had made a fascinating discovery.

After a quick snatch-and-grab during laundry day, Kate had called for Gidget to come. As usual, the Goldendoodle feigned hearing loss.

When Kate repeated the command, her elbow bumped into Gidget's bag of treats. The sound miraculously restored her dog's hearing, and Gidget took a step toward Kate. "Good girl, Gidget!" Kate said, encouraging her to come closer.

The moment the dog heard the words—maybe enhanced with the sound of possible treats—she ran to Kate.

Kate took the sock from Gidget's mouth, told her again what a good girl she was, and then tossed her a treat.

From that point forward, whenever Gidget chose to ignore a command, Kate would say "Good girl, Gidget!" and nine times out of ten the dog would obey.

In her early training, Gidget had made a connection between the words and the reward—and it had stayed with her all these years.

As Gidget stood in the kitchen with a defiant look in her eyes and a sock in her mouth, Kate simply smiled and said, "Good girl, Gidget! Come."

And she did.

Gidget walked to Kate, gave up the sock, and received a treat and a thorough bonus back scratch.

As Kate continued to praise her dog, she couldn't help but think about the benefits of early training. She was also reminded of the importance of being who you are—and believing what the one who really loves you believes about you.

PAWS & PONDER...

Today's proverb talks about directing your children toward the right path. What are some practical ways you direct your child toward the right path? Proverbs 22:6 is a principle, not a promise. What's the difference between the two? Have you done everything you can to "train up your child in the way he or she should go" only to watch them go toward the opposite path? Spend some time talking to God about that. Pray for that child today. And then ask God to help you surrender your child's faith journey to him, remembering God loves your child even more than you do!

Paws & Pray

O Father, it is so hard to watch children go their own way. I realize you know those feelings more than anyone. For those children who are struggling—who are choosing paths their family would have never chosen for them—please lead them back to you, in your perfect timing and will. And Lord, for those little ones being shown the path of life today, cement that path in their little hearts and illuminate it in their sweet souls so that its light may never dim and they may daily walk with you.

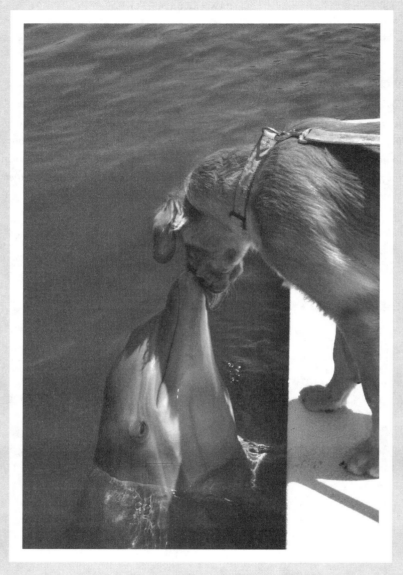

Love makes up for all offenses.

PROVERBS 10:12

69

THE SALTY KISS OF FRIENDSHIP

An intelligent heart acquires knowledge,
and the ear of the wise seeks knowledge.

PROVERBS 18:15, ESV

MARIE HAD ALWAYS LOVED DOLPHINS. From the time she was a little girl, she knew she wanted to be a dolphin trainer. After getting a degree in zoology from North Carolina State University, she was overjoyed when she was offered an internship at the Dolphin Research Center in the Florida Keys. And even happier when, just two years later, they offered her a full-time position.

During the next eight years, Marie gained invaluable insight and knowledge about the mammals she was so passionate about. And she loved sharing her passion for dolphins with visitors from all around the world.

Not only had Marie been able to encourage people to fall in love with dolphins, she also managed to share her passion and love for dolphins with her Golden retriever, Gunner.

Marie began taking Gunner to work with her when he was just a puppy. The playful Golden was fascinated with the large sea-dwelling mammals and would race down the docks to watch them swim and play in their natural lagoons.

Over time, Marie noticed that some of their resident dolphins seemed just as curious about Gunner as the rapidly growing puppy was about them. The more inquisitive dolphins would even come up for a closer look when Gunner was on the dock.

Eventually, Marie began inviting Gunner to join in some training and playtime exercises with the dolphins.

Gunner's favorite role as a canine trainer was to help retrieve toys during playtime. He took his job very seriously—walking with pride after gently taking a toy from a dolphin and bringing it to Marie.

Marie loved watching her dog's excitement when he interacted with the dolphins—especially one dolphin named Delta.

Gunner and Delta were close in age and truly seemed to consider each other a friend. At first the two watched each other from afar. But eventually Marie could tell that Gunner and Delta looked for each other. Eventually they began to play—Gunner would bring Delta's toys back to him, and Delta would jump out of the water to elicit a bark from Gunner. In fact, the two became so close that Delta would often come up out of the water to receive a kiss from Gunner—who loved giving his salty friend a good lick on the face.

Day after day, Marie was inspired by the friendship between her dog and Delta. They were two animals taking time to get to know each other. They focused more on what they had in common than on their differences and were willing to work together to build a strong and enjoyable friendship. Marie was grateful her young son, Lucas, got to witness the progression of the two animals' friendship.

When Lucas began walking and becoming more active, Marie began to wonder if perhaps her son would miss out on some of the more traditional experiences of childhood by living in the Keys, where entertainment and social opportunities were somewhat limited.

But each day as she watched her little boy stand on a dock blowing kisses to dolphins and receiving kisses from Gunner, she realized that some of the most powerful lessons are best learned in nature's classroom.

Lucas was growing up and seeing firsthand that friends can come in all shapes, sizes, and skin textures. Some friends can have two legs, some might have four, and some might have no legs at all.

Each friend mattered and had value.

And each friend deserved time to get to know the other and discover that we really aren't that different after all.

PAWS & PONDER...

Proverbs 18:15 describes the role your heart and ears play in obtaining knowledge. How do you acquire knowledge with your heart? Or seek knowledge with your ears? What roles do knowledge, intelligence, and wisdom play in being able to see past the differences you have with others and, instead, discover what you have in common?

Paws & Pray

Father God, thank you so much for creating such diversity on our planet. What a beautiful world this is with the vast array of species, each with unique characteristics. Help me not to make quick judgments of those who are different from me. I want to be someone defined by my love for you and others—a love that can only come from knowledge of you. Grant me a desire to know you even more.

70

ḢOT ḊOG!

My child, eat honey; it is good. And just as honey from the comb

is sweet on your tongue, you may be sure that wisdom is good

for the soul. Get wisdom and you have a bright future.

PROVERBS 24:13-14, GNT

TEN-YEAR-OLD LIBBY PLACED five little white cones a foot apart in a straight line. At the end of the line she stacked bricks several feet apart and laid a broom across them. Finally, she laid her old Barbie Pop-up n' Play tunnel at a ninety-degree angle to the broom.

"Perfect!" she proclaimed, running into the house to retrieve her dog, Daisy, and a red cup filled with diced hot dogs.

Using masking tape to attach the red cup to her belt, Libby was finally ready to begin Daisy's agility training. And with the smell of hot dogs in the air, the little white Havanese was more than ready!

Daisy bounced with excitement as Libby attached her pink leash to Daisy's collar and led her out the door.

Libby couldn't wait to teach Daisy how to do the agility course she had set up. After watching an agility show on Animal Planet, Libby had been inspired to create one of her own. And although Daisy had never even been to obedience school, Libby just knew her dog could be the best agility dog in the world.

The energetic little dog yipped and jumped, trying to reach the cup of hot dogs dangling from the waistband of Libby's shorts.

"You gotta earn your treats, girl," Libby explained. "First, I'll walk you through the course. And each time you do something right, I'll give ya a piece of hot dog. Soon, you'll be able to do the course without me having to show you. Okay?"

As if understanding the instructions perfectly, Daisy barked and sat at attention.

"Good girl," Libby laughed, giving the dog her first meaty morsel.

Holding Daisy's leash up high, Libby began to walk Daisy in and out of the cones, giving her a treat at every zig and zag. She then built up enough speed to jump over the broomstick. Libby was so thrilled by Daisy's flawless jump that she gave her a handful of hot dog pieces. Libby crawled through the tunnel first, then went back and carried Daisy through. Although she hadn't gone through on her own accord, Daisy was still rewarded with a treat for her trouble.

Libby and Daisy went through the obstacles at least two dozen times, with one break for Libby to refill the hot dog cup.

After an hour, Libby ran inside to ask her family to come out and watch Daisy—the world's greatest agility dog—complete the course all by herself.

Libby watched with pride as her little dog zigzagged around the ones, leapt over the broom, and scurried through the tunnel before running straight to Libby to receive a handful of meat.

Libby's dad laughed as Daisy sank to the ground, head between her paws, belly spreading out beneath her.

"Well, Libby girl, you did it!" he said proudly. "You taught Daisy how to do an agility course." Then he added with a chuckle, "And what a meat coma feels like! How many hot dogs did you feed that dog anyway?"

Libby grinned coyly, shrugging her shoulders. "As many as it took for her to learn."

PAWS & PONDER...

In what ways is wisdom good for the soul? How have you found this to be true in your own life? How does Proverbs 9:12 (see devotion 92) relate to Proverbs 24:13–14? Where does wisdom begin?

Paws & Pray

Lord, I long to be a person who is known for godly wisdom, wisdom that begins and ends with you. Help me to crave you and your Word more than anything else. Make your Word sweeter to my heart than honey—or even hot dogs!

71

ℒET ℌIM ℛIDE

Being wise is better than being strong; yes,
knowledge is more important than strength.

PROVERBS 24:5, GNT

JUDY KNEW THERE WERE MANY THINGS her son Joseph could *not* do. Countless professionals in a variety of fields had made sure she knew all about Joe's limitations. But while their assessments were valid, Judy knew that her son was so much more than the sum of his limitations—so much more than his autism diagnosis.

She also knew—believed deep in her soul—that she needed to spend her energy discovering all the things Joseph *could* do instead of focusing on the things he could not.

And so when a physical therapist suggested equine therapy to help Joseph build his motor skills and confidence, Judy jumped at the opportunity.

From the moment twelve-year-old Joseph stepped onto the therapeutic horse ranch, his face lit up.

He studied the horses and observed the riders. And he focused intently as his instructor walked him through the steps involved in preparing a horse to be rideable.

Judy's heart swelled with a mix of joy and fear as Joseph mounted a horse named Sue. She hadn't realized just how large horses were before seeing her accident-prone son on the back of one. And yet, Joseph appeared perfectly calm.

Refusing to bow to fear, Judy watched in awe as her son adjusted his hands and posture at the trainer's direction—her son who had difficulty following basic instructions.

Clearly, the trainer knew how to communicate with her son.

And over time it became equally apparent that her son knew just how to communicate with his horse, Sue.

Several months after his first riding lesson, Joseph was invited to participate in the Special Olympics in the equine sport of dressage.

Judy was unsure. She was just happy that Joseph was able to stay upright in a saddle! *Could he really handle training and performing in the Special Olympics?*

Yet once again where Judy was apprehensive, Joseph was sure.

He wanted to compete, so Judy hesitantly agreed.

The following months required extra training sessions and instruction. But Joseph seemed to be a natural. With each lesson, Judy watched her son grow in confidence and coordination as he led Sue through their dressage routine—a series of skills set to music.

When the big day finally arrived, Judy's entire family drove out to the fairgrounds to watch Joseph and Sue compete. As the family went into the arena to get their seats, Judy walked with Joseph to meet Sue's trainer and get their horse ready.

But the moment Judy saw the trainer's face she knew something was wrong.

"I'm afraid Sue won't be able to compete today," the trainer said. "She didn't handle the trip too well. She's currently trying to kick the sides out of her stall."

Judy was startled by this description of the normally placid horse.

Joseph had worked so hard to get here. She glanced at her son, wondering how he would react to this disappointing turn of events.

"I want to talk to Sue," Joe said matter-of-factly.

The trainer shook his head, saying it was too dangerous.

Joseph became insistent.

Judy asked if there was any way Joseph could at least see Sue.

"If I can get a halter on her, I'll bring her out," the trainer said. "But *only* if I can safely get her in a halter."

Judy mouthed the words *thank you.*

Twenty minutes later Sue was led out of the stall area. As soon as Joseph saw Sue he began walking toward the unhappy horse as she pulled against her lead line.

Judy started to grab her son's arm, but something gave her pause.

She watched as her son put his hands on either side of Sue's head, then lowered his head to her own. Without speaking a word, he began breathing into Sue's nostrils.

The horse stilled.

Joseph started talking to the horse in tones too soft for anyone to hear. But the results were astounding. The horse, who moments before had been agitated and unsure, suddenly was completely calm.

Joseph told the trainer that Sue needed to take a walk.

Exchanging a questioning look with the director of the riding program, the trainer agreed.

Joseph confidently walked Sue around the back of the arena.

Judy had to fight to keep her jaw closed.

Who was this boy?

After their walk, Joseph brought Sue back to the staging area.

"She's ready now," the boy declared. "She just needed a walk."

The staff of the ranch all looked to Judy.

"If you're okay with it, then let him ride," Judy said, hoping she was making the right choice.

Later that day, Judy allowed her pent-up tears to flow freely as she watched her son—the boy so many people had said would never do more than exist—win the gold medal in dressage.

He may have limitations, but Judy knew they would never stop him from doing what God had created him to do.

PAWS & PONDER . . .

Do you ever feel defined by your limitations? Have you ever considered that what the world calls a limitation may actually be a gift from God, even a strength in disguise? Take a moment and offer your weakness to God. Ask him to fill you with wisdom and vision to see beyond your limitations so you can see the plans he has for you.

Paws & Pray

Lord, I recognize that I have limitations and weaknesses. Help me not to be defined by them but to only be defined by who you say I am. God, remind me that in my weakness I am made strong in you.

72

GOOD NEWS

Good news from far away is like cold water to the thirsty.

PROVERBS 25:25

CAT AND HER HUSBAND, AL, knew their cat, Hans, needed a friend. The Ragdoll had come into their lives as a kitten and had immediately bonded with their older cat, Katie. But when Katie lost her battle with kidney disease, Hans was devastated. Hans became clingy and skittish.

At first Al was resistant to the idea of another cat—the pain of losing Katie was still so raw.

But as Hans continued to grieve the loss of his friend, Al and Cat began searching for a younger female on a local Ragdoll cat rescue site.

Unfortunately, only older male cats were available, so they decided to wait and pray for just the right cat for their family.

They didn't have to wait long.

Just a few days after their initial search, they received a message about a three-year-old female blue-point Ragdoll named Lily who was in need of a new home. Cat and Al immediately emailed the family to let them know they would love to meet Lily. And then they waited.

And waited.

Cat didn't want to get her hopes up, but at the same time she felt sure that Lily was meant to be theirs.

They prayed again, asking God to bring just the right cat into their lives—at just the right time. Then Cat and Al both went to work and tried not to think about Lily.

When they returned home, there was still no response from Lily's family.

"Perhaps they changed their minds about giving her up for adoption," Cat said.

"Maybe they chose another family for Lily," Al said.

Suddenly the phone rang, and Cat answered it. It was Lily's owner. She had been touched by Cat and Al's email and wanted to tell them what was going on.

She explained that when their son returned home from being deployed overseas, his doctor discovered he had a brain tumor.

As the family was processing this news, Hurricane Katrina hit New Orleans and destroyed their home. The family moved to North Carolina to be close to the hospital where their son was scheduled for experimental treatment.

The family had several cats, but Lily was so young that she was having trouble adjusting to all the changes. All she wanted to do was play. But her human family couldn't give her the attention and affection she deserved. They wanted her to go to a home where she could thrive, but they were struggling with the difficult decision to let her go.

Cat listened with humble gratitude for their sacrifice.

"We would like to talk it over as a family this weekend," Lily's owner said, "and then I will call you on Sunday."

And so again Cat and Al waited, fearing the answer would be no.

When the phone rang on Sunday, the answer was yes. The family wanted Cat and Al to give Lily a home. Cat tried not to squeal into the phone as arrangements were made for Lily to be brought to them that evening.

Cat scooped up Hans.

"You're going to get a little sister tonight," she told him, her voice giddy with excitement.

When Lily stepped out of her cat carrier, she began walking around the house like she belonged there. And from the moment Hans first sniffed her, he had not stopped following her around.

Lily's original owners still keep in touch. Cat sends them regular updates about the cat they loved enough to let go. And Cat is delighted every time she gets an update about their son's miraculous recovery. Not only is Lily thriving, but so are two grateful families that have been connected because of her.

PAWS & PONDER...

What good news have you experienced recently? What good news are you longing to hear? In what way is the good news of the gospel like cold water to someone who is thirsty?

---❁---

Paws & Pray

Lord Jesus, you provided the best news of all when you defeated sin and death and rose to life so that by believing and trusting in you, I can have a relationship with God. Thank you for choosing to lay down your life for me. Father, help me to be willing to share this incredible news with others.

7 3

A PICTURE OF LOYALTY

Many will say they are loyal friends,

but who can find one who is truly reliable?

PROVERBS 20:6

LOYALTY CAN BE REVEALED in a variety of ways—a friend defending another, an employer keeping his word, a faithful spouse. But to Cindy and her daughter, Abbey, loyalty looks like a white Bichon Frise named Baci.

When Abbey, the third of four children, was in elementary school, she was diagnosed with abdominal migraines, a painful condition that led to chronic vomiting every few days—often in the wee hours of the morning. Each night when Cindy heard her daughter heading for the bathroom, she jumped out of bed to join her, not wanting her to suffer alone. Baci always followed close behind.

As Cindy would hold her daughter's hair and rub her back, Baci would curl up on the floor beside the little girl. When the episode was over—usually thirty minutes later—Abbey, Cindy, and Baci would wearily climb back into their beds.

Eventually, the nightly routine began taking a toll, not just on Abbey but on Cindy as well. Her nightly vigils had resulted in extreme fatigue and exhaustion.

One night, Cindy slept through Abbey's nightly run to the bathroom. When she awoke the next morning, she was consumed with guilt.

"Oh, Abbey, honey, I am so sorry I wasn't there for you," she apologized over breakfast.

Abbey's sweet smile warmed Cindy's heart. "It's okay, Mommy. Baci was with me."

Cindy's expression gave away her disbelief because Abbey nodded and added, "Baci followed me into the bathroom and lay down next to me till I was all done."

Cindy picked up the fluffy little hero and gave her a kiss of gratitude on the head.

It wasn't the only night Baci was there for Abbey when she was sick. In fact, it happened numerous times over the next few months.

On more than one occasion, when Cindy did wake up and would start running toward the bathroom, she would be met by a sleepy Baci heading back to her dog bed, after seeing Abbey safely back to her human bed.

Baci had already handled it.

Baci's actions and her unwavering loyalty were a comfort to a sick girl and her exhausted mother—keeping one from feeling alone, while allowing the other to get the rest her body desperately needed.

Thankfully now, ten years later, those sleepless nights and abdominal migraines are a distant memory. And sweet Baci is still providing companionship and loyalty to her most grateful family.

PAWS & PONDER...

What does loyalty look like to you? Who is your most loyal friend? How can you show loyalty to a friend today?

Paws & Pray

God, you have given me so many examples of what loyalty looks like. I see instances of loyalty throughout your Word, in my relationships, and even in the animals I love. And yet, there is no one as loyal as you. I marvel at your steadfast love for me. Help me to look for ways to demonstrate your loyalty and love to others. And enable me to be a truly loyal friend.

Do not rejoice when your enemy meets trouble.

PROVERBS 24:17, TLB

74

WHAT HAPPENED TO YOUR CAT?

The words of the reckless pierce like swords,

but the tongue of the wise brings healing.

PROVERBS 12:18, NIV

CAROL BASKED IN THE WARMTH of the afternoon sun at the park. It seemed everyone was enjoying the weather. The normally quiet park was abuzz with activity as fellow sunseekers jogged, walked, and pushed strollers along the tree-lined pathways.

"Doesn't the sun feel good, Sephy?" Carol said, winding her cat's leash around her hand.

The outdoor excursions were leisurely and relaxing, allowing Sephy time to attack a clump of grass or roll around on the sidewalk, and provided the two of them a change of scenery and some fresh air.

As Carol watched Sephy explore, she heard someone say, "What a little cutie pie you are!"

As the woman knelt next to the little tabby, Sephy did what came naturally. She began purring and rubbing against the woman's leg. Then she flopped down and rolled onto her back for a tummy rub.

"You're so sweet," the woman said, laughing.

Sephy was just getting started with her repertoire of tricks. As she rolled back over and got up to demonstrate her ninja-like moves and pounce on a stick, Carol thought, *I never get tired of seeing this.*

But when she heard a gasp from the woman, Carol mentally prepared herself for the words she knew would come next.

"Oh my goodness, what happened to your cat's tail?" the woman asked, quickly standing up and backing away.

I really need to get a T-shirt printed so I don't have to keep saying this, Carol silently lamented.

"Actually, nothing happened. She's a bobtail—a breed known for their short stubby little tails. Her tail just happens to be extra short— almost like a little nub," she said, wiggling the tip of her thumb in the air.

The woman kept staring at Persephone's back end. "The poor little thing! How awful." The pity in her voice was unmistakable.

Ouch.

Carol's grip tightened on Sephy's leash as the little ninja made her way to the sidewalk.

After completing a perfect roll, Sephy turned toward the woman and waited to receive another belly rub.

Instead, the woman gave Sephy a quick pat on the head, told Carol to have a nice day, and then left.

Sephy looked at the retreating woman, then back at Carol, her little head cocked slightly to the side. It was as if she were saying, "Why didn't she pet me longer? Did I do something bad?" Carol was used to this reaction from strangers, but it was frustrating to see Sephy's confusion. How was Sephy supposed to understand people showering her with attention one minute and then suddenly disappearing when they noticed she was different?

If Sephy's response is any indication, I can't even imagine how hurt I would be if someone rejected me for being different.

"Just because she's different doesn't mean there's anything wrong with her," Carol almost shouted out loud.

She scooped up Sephy and whispered in her ear, "You are the cutest, most talented and wonderful cat in the world. I love you." Carol kissed the tip of Sephy's nose. "And personally, I think tails are highly overrated."

Sephy rubbed her head against Carol's cheek.

After a few minutes of reassuring cuddles, Carol put Sephy down on the grass to continue prowling.

"Way to go, sweetie! Don't ever stop being you."

PAWS & PONDER...

Has your heart ever been pierced by reckless words? Or felt healing from wise words? Why do words hold so much power? What words are you longing to hear today?

Paws & Pray

Father, would you speak your words over me today? I want your words of truth to be louder than any other words I hear. Lord, please heal the wounds I've been carrying from other people's words. Put your words in my mouth that I can share them with others.

7 5

OFF LEASH

The wise in heart accept commands,

but a chattering fool comes to ruin.

PROVERBS 10:8, NIV

KATHY LOVED ALLOWING HER DOG, Pepper, to walk off leash as much as possible. The Australian shepherd was the most obedient and compliant dog Kathy had ever had, and Kathy trusted her completely whether she was attached to a leash or not.

Pepper would heel next to Kathy, never running after squirrels or chasing deer or darting off to play with other dogs.

Several times a week, Kathy and Pepper would head to nearby trails. Kathy loved watching Pepper prance by her side with her entire back end wagging and ears flipped forward, evidence of how delighted she was to be free and enjoying the outdoors with her owner.

One day as they were walking—Pepper off her leash and Kathy enjoying a time of prayer—Kathy noticed a large dog charging toward them, with its owner being pulled behind it. The owner still was holding the dog's leash, but he could not restrain his dog. Fearing what might happen if the dog decided to charge Pepper, Kathy clipped the leash onto Pepper's collar. Pepper looked up at Kathy as if to ask, "Why are you restraining me? You know I'll be good."

Kathy did trust her dog, but she did not trust the dog rapidly approaching them. The man repeatedly called his dog's name as he tried in vain to get the dog to stop.

Kathy used the leash to move Pepper to the other side of her—away from the out-of-control dog.

Then Kathy steered Pepper to the far side of the trail, shortened her hold on the leash, and walked quickly past the man and his dog.

"Sorry about that," the man said sheepishly, finally halting his dog. "We're working with a trainer, but this big boy still has a way to go."

Kathy smiled politely, wished him well, and she and Pepper continued on their way. Kathy kept Pepper on the leash as a precaution.

Pepper again glanced up at Kathy, her big brown eyes full of questions she could never ask. She didn't pull against the leash, hoping Kathy would release her for the rest of the walk. She took her cues from Kathy and trusted that she knew best.

PAWS & PONDER...

How do you respond to a command? Eagerly or reluctantly? Why is it difficult to accept a command when you don't understand the reason behind it? How can trust help you better accept the commands you don't understand?

Paws & Pray

Lord, help me to trust you enough to accept your commands without grumbling, even when I don't understand your reasons. Forgive me for all the times I thought my way was best, rattling off a list of excuses about why I couldn't follow your directives. God, I know you are good and look out for me. Help me to trust you and obey your commands always.

76

A RUDE AWAKENING

It is dangerous to have zeal without knowledge,
and the one who acts hastily makes poor choices.

PROVERBS 19:2, NET

OVER THE YEARS JAN AND PAUL'S dogs had acquired quite a rap sheet with the local police department. The black Labs, Jack and Piper, loved escaping the confines of their fenced-in yard—only to run straight to the police station less than a mile away and turn themselves in.

The Labs' escapades were the topic of many conversations—and quite a few laughs—among Jan and Paul's family, friends, and colleagues.

But sadly, just a few years after his first run-in with local law enforcement, Jack passed away.

And as if desperate to find her best friend, Piper became obsessed with escaping.

Piper had always had a talent for finding any and all weak spots along the fence line, but after losing Jack she became single-minded in searching for other ways to get through the wooden barrier.

Piper would find some loose slats and push herself through or shimmy her body through a small gap in the gate.

Keeping an eye on Piper had become a constant battle.

One morning, several months after losing Jack, Jan got up before sunrise to attend an early-morning Bible study. Not wanting to disturb her husband or Piper, who was sleeping in the hallway just outside their room, Jan quietly snuck out of the house, locking the front door of their hundred-year-old farmhouse behind her.

Unbeknownst to Jan, Piper decided to follow. Maybe she wanted to go with Jan, search for Jack, or just enjoy the sunrise. That morning, Piper added another trick to her skill set: pawing at the handle on the front door until the lock disengaged, and the door popped open. At least, that's what Jan and Paul would surmise.

Not long after Jan left for Bible study, a neighbor called the police concerned that Jan and Paul's front door was wide open, and their dog was wandering around the front yard.

Two police officers arrived quickly and found everything as the neighbor described.

The officers cautiously entered the house with Piper following close behind.

The officers searched the house and eventually came to Jan and Paul's bedroom—where Paul was still sound asleep!

"Sir? Sir!" shouted the officer standing closest to Paul. He shined his flashlight in Paul's eyes. "Sir! Are you okay?"

Paul sat straight up in bed, startled awake. He tried to make sense of the scene before him.

Why are the police in my room?

Where is Jan?

Why are they asking if I'm okay?

So many questions.

And one very affectionate dog licking the officer's hand.

Piper. *Of course.*

After assuring the officers he was fine, Paul quickly grabbed his robe and saw the officers to the door.

An hour later Jan returned home.

"Janis!" she heard Paul bellow as she walked in the door. "You left the front door ajar. You are never going to believe what *your* dog did!"

Jan protested her innocence. "What did Piper do this time?"

As Paul recounted his early-morning police welfare check and wake-up call, Jan could barely keep from laughing.

After hearing the story, Jan got ready for work and on her way out, she made sure the door was securely closed behind her. She hadn't been at the office long before the phone rang. It was Paul.

"Piper escaped again—on her own. I'm sorry I blamed you. We'll both need to take extra measures."

From that day on, Jan and Paul made sure the front door was closed and bolted when they left the house, much to Piper's dismay.

PAWS & PONDER...

Have you ever made a poor choice because of a hasty decision? What was the result? Can you think of a current example of someone exhibiting zeal without knowledge? How might haste cause problems for yourself and others? How can you guard against making hasty decisions?

Paws & Pray

Lord, help me to think before I act. Direct my thoughts to you—who you are, what you have done, and what you would have me do. Help me pause to pray, consult your Word, and seek counsel from others so that I do not act rashly and regret it later.

77

ELSA WON'T LET GO

Joyful are those who listen to me, watching for me daily at

my gates, waiting for me outside my home!

PROVERBS 8:34

THE FIRST TIME ASHLEY DROVE home from the grocery store and found her white Akita, Elsa, sitting in the front yard, she didn't think much of it. She had left their two-year-old dog inside the house, but Ashley assumed her husband had let the dog out just before she got home. When Ashley opened the car door, Elsa leapt onto her lap. Her happy cries and sounds made Ashley laugh.

The next time Ashley drove up to find Elsa sitting by the driveway, she asked her husband how long Elsa had been outside. "She started whining as soon as you left so I let her outside." Then, looking a bit sheepish, he added, "I forgot she was there."

The third time Ashley pulled up to find Elsa sitting at attention at the top of the driveway, she suspected her dog was actually waiting for her.

Ashley shouldn't have been surprised—after all, Elsa waited for her outside the bathroom door, lay at her feet when she was working on her computer or at her desk, and slept on the floor next to her side of the bed at night. But Elsa's front-yard vigil deeply touched Ashley's heart.

Something about her dog choosing to wait outside for her, ignoring all the distractions on their street, and then racing to greet her the minute she got out of her vehicle made Ashley choke up.

Elsa was the picture of loyalty and devotion.

Over the next few months, whenever Ashley left and someone else was home, Elsa would whine at the back door until she was allowed outside to sit vigil for Ashley's return.

It got to the point that Elsa could identify Ashley's car from six houses away.

Her eyes were always searching for it, her ears listening for the voice of the human she adored.

Elsa became Ashley's living, breathing, tail-wagging picture of what it looks like to wait in anticipation and joy for God—waiting for him to answer a prayer, waiting for him to reveal his plan, watching for evidences of his grace. The loyal dog also served as a beautiful picture of the delight God surely feels when his beloved children come home to him.

PAWS & PONDER...

Are you waiting on God for something? Are you waiting in joyful anticipation? Or does your wait feel more like a burden? What evidences of God's grace have you seen recently—either in your life or someone else's?

Paws & Pray

Father, thank you for loving me. Thank you for delighting in each one of your children and rejoicing when a person comes to faith through your Son. God, because you love me, I know I can trust you—even when the waiting is long. Fill my heart with joy and anticipation as I wait and hope in you.

78

ƎNOUGH

Give me neither poverty nor riches! Give me just enough to satisfy my

needs. For if I grow rich, I may deny you and say, "Who is the LORD?"

And if I am too poor, I may steal and thus insult God's holy name.

PROVERBS 30:8-9

KATHRYN WATCHED from the kitchen window as the cat she had seen off and on in their backyard made his way to their patio. His gray coat almost perfectly matched the overcast sky.

After first spotting the animal through her bedroom window several months earlier, Kathryn had made it her mission to befriend the stray she nicknamed Shadow.

She started by leaving a can of tuna at the edge of the woods where he seemed to disappear every day—despite her husband's caution that the food would only attract raccoons and opossums. Over time Kathryn moved the cans closer and closer to their house.

Eventually, Shadow began eating breakfast and dinner on the patio.

Occasionally, when the weather was particularly bad, Kathryn would open the door to their laundry room and invite him inside.

"You're allergic, remember?" her husband would remind her.

Kathryn would smile and say, "Yes, but he can stay in the laundry room—until the storm passes. I'll block it off from the rest of the house."

However, Shadow never did accept her invitation to come into their home. Kathryn wasn't going to give up and came up with another plan. The few nights when the temperature dropped below freezing, she cracked the garage door open and made a little bed for Shadow out of a cardboard box filled with old flannel sheets. And while she never saw him in the box, she would discover remnants of fur and leaves on the sheets that assured her he had spent some time out of the elements.

As Kathryn continued to watch the cat walk through the yard, she smiled. Shadow found a sunny spot on the patio and began grooming himself, oblivious to Kathryn's gaze. Knowing Shadow was comfortable and content, she returned her focus to the three-layer cake she was icing for her twin daughters' birthday party. She really wanted the party to be special, but she still needed to pick up party favors, balloons, a piñata, and a few more gifts. She hurried to finish so she could stop at the store before picking up the twins. As she went through her mental list of party supplies and gifts, a thought went through her mind.

Was it enough?

Her daughters' friends all had such elaborate parties, and Kathryn felt the need to try and keep up—for the twins' sake.

Kathryn piped *Happy Birthday* on the top of the cake and placed it in a cake container. She grabbed her purse and as she walked out the back door, she stopped to pet Shadow. The cat accepted her touch with a purr. His food bowl was empty. "You must have enjoyed that Seafood Delight for breakfast," Kathryn said. Shadow got up, arched his back as he stretched his front legs, then jumped up on his favorite chair, curling up on the cushion.

"You sure don't need much to make you happy, do ya, buddy?" Kathryn said, scratching his head as she left.

Her words, spoken as a simple observation, stayed with her throughout the day. They drifted through her mind as she walked up and down the Target aisles looking unsuccessfully for party favors and a piñata. The words continued to swirl around her consciousness as the birthday girls filled balloons with confetti as a substitute for the piñata and put ribbons on small stuffed animals to use as favors. That evening, ten twelve-year-old girls laughed, played, and ate cake, happy to simply be together.

As Kathryn opened a can of food for Shadow that night, she thought about the cat who was content with so little. All he needed was food, warmth, and affection. Those essentials were enough for him, even though she offered him more—an entire laundry room full of more.

Kathryn placed the food on the patio, and she was surprised when Shadow rubbed against her legs before starting to devour the meal.

"Well, you're very welcome," she said softly.

Shadow purred as he ate, clearly enjoying his dinner as much as he had his breakfast.

"This really is enough for you, isn't it, little guy?"

Kathryn could see her daughters dancing with their friends in the family room, their faces aglow with joy.

She stroked Shadow's back. "You know what?" she said, the realization warming her heart. "It is for me too."

PAWS & PONDER...

Do you ever struggle with the concept of *enough*? Having enough? Being enough? Doing enough? It is so easy to feel *less than* in a world that screams more, more, more. Take a minute to write down any areas in which you are experiencing discontentment or a feeling of *not enough*. Confess those to the Lord and ask him to remind you of his sufficiency and love.

Paws & Pray

Lord, you are enough. Remind me of this truth and fill my spirit daily with an awareness of you. Help me be content with all I have in you.

Let the wise hear and increase in learning, and the one who understands obtain guidance.

PROVERBS 1:5, ESV

79

𝒜 GOOD 𝒩AME

A good name is more desirable than great riches;

to be esteemed is better than silver or gold.

PROVERBS 22:1, NIV

"DARCY!"

With one word—the name of her very best friend—the two-year-old Golden retriever named Gracie woke from a sound sleep.

"Want to see Darcy?" Jen, her human, asked, her voice rising an octave on the last syllable.

Gracie stood up, vigorously shook herself from nose to tail, then immediately broke into her "Darcy dance." She ran from window to window looking for her best canine friend. She pawed at the door. She spun in tight circles. She jumped at the knob on the back door, willing someone to take pity on her and open it.

Gracie simply could not wait to get to Darcy, the ten-year-old Portuguese water dog who lived across the street. The two had been friends since Gracie was a puppy and Darcy towered over her. Now the two dogs stood shoulder to shoulder. And although they differed in age and breed, the two had been best friends since they first sniffed each other more than two years ago.

"So, I take it you *do* want to see Darcy?" Jen teased.

Gracie barked her answer, scratching frantically at the door until Jen opened it. Gracie bounded from the back deck to the yard in one leap and ran around the corner to the front of the house. She ran to the end of the driveway where she sat in rapt attention, awaiting the first glimpse of her friend.

Watching Gracie's anxious anticipation brought a sweet memory to the forefront of Jen's mind—one of her beloved granddad. She had adored both of her grandparents, but both were gone now. It still made Jen tear up when special memories of them came to mind. The bond she shared with her granddad had been especially strong.

As a little girl, Jen couldn't have imagined anyone stronger, smarter, or more talented than him. He could build anything, fix anything, and make anyone laugh—especially her. As a young girl, she once told him that he was stronger than Superman and nicer than Santa Claus. He was a simple and humble man who worked hard to earn a modest living for his family, but to his granddaughter he was more important than royalty.

I was just like you, Gracie, she thought with a smile. *Waiting at the front door for my best friend to pull into the driveway.*

Now Gracie was standing in the driveway, looking across the street. Darcy was with her human, just outside their front door. Gracie's back end started to wiggle. With raised ears, an outstretched tail, and straight back, she was the picture of controlled energy.

But the moment Darcy's owner released her to cross the street and she stepped onto Gracie's driveway, the Golden's energy was released, and the dogs leapt toward each other with their version of a hug before engaging in a high-speed game of chase. They streaked across the yard, barking happily, then sporadically came to an abrupt halt to sniff the ground and then each other before repeating the cycle.

Jen laughed as she watched their antics. Yet the memory of her granddad still lingered in her mind. As Gracie ran circles of sheer joy around Darcy, Jen could almost feel her granddad wrap her in a bear hug.

"I love you, too," she whispered, wrapping her arms tightly around her middle.

A moment later Darcy's owner approached from one direction, and the two dogs ran toward Jen from the other direction, inviting her to romp with them. Granddad would have approved.

PAWS & PONDER . . .

Why is a good name better than riches? What kinds of attributes give someone a good name? Who would you consider to be someone with a "good name"? What is it about that person that made you select them? What do you hope people think about when they hear your name?

Paws & Pray

Lord, help me to pursue a good name over fame and riches. Let me be known for my integrity, love, humility, and kindness. Lord, your name is the greatest name of all. Thank you for being an example I can emulate.

80

ᴅOES ᴉT ᴄOUNT?

As a dog returns to its vomit, so a fool repeats his foolishness.

PROVERBS 26:11

BARBARA STROKED her German shepherd's head with her left hand, while cradling the phone with her right.

"Oh, Coco, please don't get sick," she pleaded, while waiting for someone from the after-hours vet's office to answer.

Her one-year-old shepherd had found a box of crayons in her daughter's backpack—the backpack she continually told her daughter to hang up—and begun to devour them. The moment Barbara walked into the kitchen and saw the colorful remnants on the floor, her heart sank.

Are crayons poisonous to dogs? She examined the box, which said "nontoxic." But she didn't know whether that applied to dogs.

Barbara wrestled half an orange crayon from Coco's jaws before grabbing the few crayons Coco hadn't gotten to. Barbara eyed Coco, waiting for her to get sick at any moment.

But she needed a professional opinion on what to do.

After explaining the situation to the veterinary assistant on the phone, Barbara was assured that crayons were not poisonous, but Coco would likely begin vomiting the foreign objects.

"You'll need to keep count of how many times she throws up," the veterinary assistant said. Barbara nearly choked on the water she had just swallowed.

"If it's more than ten times within an hour, you will need to bring her in immediately," the assistant stated.

"Thank you for your help," Barbara said as she hung up the phone. Then reality hit her.

Great, Barbara bemoaned. *Vincente is away on business; I have two kids who need dinner and homework help before going to bed; it's sleeting outside; and I have a massive deadline at work. Why wouldn't I want to count how many times my dog vomits?*

An hour later, while Barbara was making dinner, Coco got sick. As Barbara cleaned it up, she began a mental count. *One.*

Coco immediately threw up again. *Two.*

Barbara cleaned it up and put the dinner ingredients away. *One night of eating cereal for dinner won't hurt the kids.*

Coco seemed to settle down. She drank some water, pawed at her tennis ball, and then lay down under the table.

After the kids finished eating, Barbara helped her daughter with her math assignment and her son with spelling homework. Coco was downstairs while Barbara tucked her kids into bed.

As she descended the stairs, anxious to finish her proposal for work, she heard the unmistakable sound of a dog heaving. She ran for the paper towels. The roll was empty.

"Coco, stay," she commanded, running to the laundry room for a new roll.

Three, she added to her mental tally.

When she returned, she was horrified to discover the mess was gone. "Gross, Coco! Ew!"

Within a few minutes Coco got sick again.

Four.

"Wait . . ." Barbara said aloud. "Does that one count? Or is that one a result of number three?"

While she was debating the eligibility of the new mess, Coco got sick again. Barbara had to race to the dog to clean it up.

"Coco, stop!" she snapped. "I can only count real ones. I don't think re-barfs count."

For the rest of the evening, Coco was on a short leash connected to

Barbara's wrist, with a roll of paper towels beside her on the sofa and a notepad on the table.

There were seven numbers and two question marks on the notepad by midnight when Coco finally fell asleep and slept soundly through the night.

The next afternoon when Barbara's children came home from school and started to drop their backpacks in the hallway, she held up a roll of paper towels and pointed to Coco. "You leave the backpacks out, you will clean it up."

With wide eyes, her kids looked from her, to the dog, to the roll of paper towels. They carefully hung their backpacks on the hooks, making sure nothing had fallen out of either one.

PAWS & PONDER . . .

Unfortunately, even when we know something is not good for us, we often return to it. What habit or destructive pattern are you struggling to overcome? When do you find yourself most tempted to return to it? God promises to help us overcome even the most gripping temptation. Give God your struggle today and ask him to help you walk away from it. Consider also talking to a counselor or a trusted godly friend who can help hold you accountable.

Paws & Pray

Lord, help me to break the habits and patterns that separate me from you and the plans you have for me. So often when life gets hard, I gravitate toward other things instead of turning to you. Forgive me, Lord. I know you are the only one who can truly satisfy and fill my hungry soul.

8 1

STOP TIGER!

Watch your tongue and keep your mouth shut,

and you will stay out of trouble.

PROVERBS 21:23

CINDY, A LONGTIME VOLUNTEER at an animal shelter, had just started her shift when the manager asked her to take the short, stocky dog for a walk.

"Of course," Cindy said, grabbing a collar and leash. "I haven't really met Tiger, so it will be a perfect way for us to get acquainted." The shelter was in a strip mall, located not far from railroad tracks. Cindy and Tiger headed to a grassy area in the direction of the train tracks.

Suddenly, the blaring whistle of the train startled both of them, and Tiger began frantically thrashing, backing away from the noise.

Before Cindy could react, Tiger had slipped out of his collar.

Cindy stood frozen, a leash and empty collar dangling from her hand. Tiger stared back at her, not realizing he was free from her control.

"Tiger . . . stay," she said slowly and assertively, attempting not to show her rising panic.

The dog shook his head, then turned around and began running back the way they had come.

"Tiger, stop!" Cindy screamed, trying to close the gap between them. *How can those little legs run so fast?*

"Tiger!" she yelled again.

Miraculously the dog headed right back to the strip mall, but when Tiger reached the entrance of a toy store, the automatic doors opened and he darted right in.

"I am so getting fired," Cindy muttered, following him inside.

Like a drill sergeant, she began shouting orders to everyone she saw. "There's a loose dog in here. His name is Tiger. Help me get him!" She pointed to one person. "You! Block that aisle."

Then another. "You! Head over there."

Then she saw Tiger dash around a corner. "Here, Tiger. Come here, boy."

A group of animated children and their parents gathered around her in the aisle. "You distract him, and I'll grab him," Cindy instructed.

Within minutes Cindy had a line of children following her. Great! She could already envision the headlines the next morning: Hysterical Pied Piper Chases Runaway Dog through Toy Store.

With a roundup crew of store employees, confused parents, and excited children, Cindy made her move. Thankfully, Tiger had worn himself out and had collapsed near the stuffed animals. But as if preparing to wrestle a crocodile, Cindy's adrenaline took over and she threw herself on top of the overweight, exhausted dog.

"You got him! You got Tiger!" a chorus of children shouted while adults clapped and cheered. Everyone crowded around Tiger and Cindy.

"Thanks, everyone. You were such a big help," Cindy said with a smile as the children got down on the floor by Tiger.

They eagerly petted him, rubbed his belly, and scratched his ears.

After putting Tiger's collar back on and making sure it was securely buckled, Cindy attached the leash and led the heavily panting dog out of the store.

"There you are!" Lisa, the manager of the animal shelter, said as Cindy and Tiger entered the lobby. "I was starting to get worried about you two."

As Cindy filled Lisa in on Tiger's adventurous game of chase, the manager's eyes widened.

"Cindy, did anyone tell you why Tiger was surrendered to us two days ago?"

Cindy shook her head.

"He bit a child."

Cindy stared at her for a moment. She looked from Lisa to the dog to the door she had just walked through.

Cindy sputtered her response, struggling to get any words to come out. "So . . . um . . . what you're saying is that I let a child-biting dog into a toy store full of children? And then asked those children to help me catch the dog?"

Not knowing whether to laugh or cry, Cindy was ready to face the music. "I am so fired, aren't I?"

"Well, your adventure with Tiger had a happy and bite-free ending," Lisa said, and both of them burst out laughing with relief.

"You're a volunteer, remember? I can't fire you," Lisa said. "But perhaps it would be best if someone else walks Tiger from now on."

"Absolutely!" Cindy agreed. "Tiger, it was nice to meet you, but let's never do this again, okay?"

The two women laughed all the way to Tiger's kennel. His great adventure ended with him curling up in the corner and falling fast asleep.

PAWS & PONDER . . .

Thankfully, Tiger kept his mouth shut while he was in the toy store. And while most people don't bite others with their teeth, our mouths can still get us in trouble. Have you ever gotten into trouble because of something you said? How might things have turned out differently if you had kept your mouth shut? The next time you feel yourself tempted to blurt out something you know you shouldn't, run your words by God first and ask him if you should say them.

Paws & Pray

Lord, my words can get me into so much trouble. Help me not only to think before I speak, but also to think of you before I speak. Bring to mind any hurtful words I've said recently so that I can confess them to you and be forgiven. And help me to speak words that will make a difference in someone's life.

82

ℒITTLE ℭESAR

We may make our plans, but God has the last word.

PROVERBS 16:1, GNT

EMILY KNEW EXACTLY the kind of dog her family needed: a medium to large breed with a temperament calm enough to be a good companion for their aging dog, Sadie, but energetic enough to make a good playmate for her two young boys.

Encouraged to visit the local humane society facility where her friend Julie volunteered, Emily and her family went in search of their new dog.

The first canine they encountered was a small terrier-mix that was barking incessantly in his crate. His bark set Emily's teeth on edge. The noise, his crazed look, and his small size eliminated him as a possibility in Emily's mind. She crossed him off the list and kept walking.

Next, they headed toward several rooms where rows of kennels and crates provided temporary housing for dogs in need of a permanent home. Emily's family members played with several large-breed dogs. But none was a good fit. Either the dogs needed a home without other animals, couldn't be trusted around children, or were too old. Emily really wanted a younger dog, one who would be there for her boys when Sadie was gone.

Emily felt discouraged. She had been certain they would find their new dog at the shelter.

As Emily's family prepared to leave, her friend Julie brought out the terrier-mix they had seen when they first arrived.

"His name is Cesar and he was found living on the streets. Would you like to spend some time with him before you go?"

I'm sorry you've had a hard life, Cesar, but you're not right for our family, Emily thought.

As she opened her mouth to say no, her oldest son said yes.

Cesar could be described in one word: wild. He ran in circles around Julie, almost knocking Emily's son over in the process. He barked, he jumped, and much to Emily's chagrin, the dog lifted his leg on her son's pant leg.

Yet as wild as he was, he was also playful, full of personality, and quite funny. He was like sunshine wrapped in fur. And although Emily kept reiterating their need for a larger dog, Julie suggested taking Cesar home for a trial stay. The shelter had recently implemented a program where prospective adoptive families could take a dog home on Friday and bring him back on Tuesday, in order to get a better idea of how the dog would fit into their family.

From the moment Cesar entered their home, he seemed to fit. He sat at Emily's feet as she prepared dinner. He followed Sadie around, even getting her to play a little bit with him. And he made the boys giggle continually with his antics. They had only known life with a senior dog, but Cesar played with the boys until they all collapsed from exhaustion.

When Tuesday came, the boys begged Emily to let them keep Cesar—even offering to pay the adoption fee from their Christmas and birthday money. But Emily still had doubts. After all, Cesar could not have been more different from the picture she had in her mind of their next dog.

And yet, something about Cesar's large brown eyes and fun-loving personality had won her heart.

"Yes, we can keep him."

Several months later, when they lost Sadie, Cesar helped mend their broken hearts. The little dog seemed to sense what each person in the family needed—sleeping with the boys, snuggling with Emily on the sofa, sitting quietly with her husband as he worked. Cesar was always there. Always ready to love and protect his family.

He might not have been the dog Emily would have chosen, but clearly God knew he was the exact dog her family needed.

PAWS & PONDER...

Have you ever been convinced of something only to discover God had something totally different in mind for you? How did your feelings change throughout that process? Did you joyfully submit right away to his will? Or did it take a while for you to accept it? Have you accepted it? Why is knowing who God is vital in being able to accept his will and plans for your life?

Paws & Pray

Lord, knowing who you are—your goodness and mercy, your righteousness and love—helps me to accept your will, especially when it is different from my own. And yet, even when I know you well, I can still struggle with accepting your will. Father, help me to trust you today more than I trusted you yesterday. Help me to trust that your plans are good, even when they don't feel good or seem to fit me. Let me believe that you are for me and not against me.

I am teaching you today—yes, you—

so you will trust in the Lord.

PROVERBS 22:19

83

CONVINCING RAVEN

I am teaching you today—yes, you—

so you will trust in the LORD.

PROVERBS 22:19

RAVEN HAD NO IDEA she could swim. The black flat-coated retriever had no idea she had come from a long line of swimmers and champion dock divers. Or how doggie-paddling was woven into her DNA. All she knew was leg-shaking, tail-tucking fear when she stood in front of a body of water.

And yet, her family knew she could swim. They knew about her bloodlines and her breed's natural love of the water. And they believed in her ability, even though she had not yet discovered it.

Each time Raven's family took her to the state park near their home, they hiked up to the lake, hoping this would be the time she would overcome her fear.

They had tried everything over the two years since they'd brought her home. They would toss sticks in the water, which she would gladly chase after—until the water got to her chest, at which point she would hightail it back to the shore. Anne had purchased a life vest for Raven, thinking that would make a difference.

It didn't.

On this outing, Anne's husband, Daniel, had carried Raven into the lake, vowing to hold her and let her get used to the feel of the water.

She clawed her way out of his arms, used his head as a springboard, and jumped back to shore.

Their children, fourteen-year-old Jackson and eleven-year-old Rachel, had even gotten in the lake and demonstrated the doggie-paddle for Raven.

But Raven wanted no part of this experiment.

"Maybe it's just not worth it," Daniel mumbled the following evening. "So Raven doesn't swim. Is that really such a big deal?"

Anne wanted to agree with him. Raven didn't need to know how to swim. It wasn't like they lived on a houseboat and she needed to learn to swim in case she accidentally fell overboard. There were many other things Raven loved—walks, playing ball, catching Frisbees.

But they had seen how much their other dogs had loved swimming and knew what a good exercise it was. Anne wanted to convince Raven of her own ability and, more important, to teach her that she could overcome her fear.

Anne knew firsthand how much fear could cost someone.

How many places had her intense fear of flying kept her from visiting? How many sleepless nights had her fear of something bad happening to her children cost her? And how many opportunities had she lost to her fear of failure?

Anne wanted more for her dog. And for herself.

The next weekend, Anne's family once again took Raven to the lake. But this time, they brought a different helper—Raven's best canine friend, Lady, an avid swimmer.

The moment Lady saw the water, she bounded in. Raven, caught up in chasing her friend, followed Lady into the lake but quickly put on the brakes once the water got deeper. Lady glanced at Raven as if to say, "C'mon. What are you waiting for?"

Lady swam over to Raven, whose feet were rooted to the rocky bottom.

Lady barked. Then play-bowed. And then leapt around, splashing and swimming back and forth in front of Raven.

Raven looked at the shore.

"You can do it, girl. Just try," Anne whispered from the shore, not knowing whether she was encouraging her dog or herself.

Raven looked back at Lady.

Anne could see the longing in her dog's eyes. The familiar look of yearning warring with fear.

Anne held her breath as Raven's front legs began to move.

She grabbed her husband's arm as the retriever's back legs left the rocky bottom.

And she whooped and hollered as her dog began the most hilarious doggie-paddle she had ever seen.

With her front legs completely straight, she kicked them up and down in what looked like a high-stepping march.

But the more time Raven spent in the water with her friend, the more relaxed she (and her swimming style) became. In less than twenty minutes, the dog who had been terrified of the water was swimming side by side with her best buddy.

"You did it!" Anne praised Raven when the dogs emerged from the lake.

Anne hugged Raven close and then hugged Lady, two dripping-wet friends.

"Thank you for being out there with my girl," she told Lady. "She trusted you, and you didn't let her down."

As Anne stood up, she looked heavenward and made a commitment to God.

"I'm willing to try, too, because I know I can trust you."

PAWS & PONDER...

What fear has you shaking on the shore? What is it you are afraid will happen if you step into the water? Take a moment to write down your fear. Next to that fear write down everything you know to be true of God. God is bigger than any fear you will ever have. And he is right there with you. Remind yourself you can trust God. He is holding you, even now. And he will never let you go.

Paws & Pray

Lord, fear distorts my vision. Fear causes me to see it as bigger than you. God, lift my eyes toward you today. Lift my head up and allow me to see things clearly. Allow me to see you as greater than anything. Enable me to take the first steps of faith toward you. I trust you, Father.

84

UNLIKELY FRIENDS

Rich and poor have this in common:
The LORD is the Maker of them all.

PROVERBS 22:2, NIV

THE SPRING AIR WAS THICK with tension as two animals, vastly different in size and temperament, warily crept toward each other. Stopping three feet apart, they froze. Not a muscle twitch nor a flick of the tail could be detected.

The show-worthy Golden retriever named Bailey stared intently at the scruffy cat recently dubbed Foxy.

"Mama, are they gonna be friends?" eight-year-old Ella whispered.

"Shhh . . . " her brother Andrew commanded.

"They'll be okay," Jen spoke softly, hoping she was right. "We just need to let them say hello."

The family had been working toward this moment for weeks—ever since discovering the stray cat in the drainage ditch at the front of their property. Over time, as the cat began losing her fear of the humans who offered her turkey and tuna and milk, she ventured closer and closer to their back door. That fact seemed to highly offend Bailey—who would bark viciously at the strange creature on the deck.

The kids didn't want to disturb the skittish cat, so they forced poor Bailey to go out on a leash through the front door every time she needed to take care of business.

"Poor dog. She can't even run in her own yard anymore," Darrell,

Bailey's human dad, observed one evening. "I think it's time the animals meet so poor Bay can have her yard back."

After much protesting, the family resolved to arrange a meeting.

But now, sensing the potential energy building in her dog, Jen was second-guessing the meet and greet.

If the cat runs off, the kids are going to be devastated, she thought, fully aware of the fact that her kids had prayed for a cat for years.

She was just about to pull Bailey back, when the cat casually walked over and rubbed her head against the broad-chested Golden. As if under a trance, Bailey stood motionless, her head cocked to the side. The cat rubbed against Bailey's side. She nuzzled her head against Bailey's back legs. She even walked under the eighty-pound dog!

Jen heard her daughter suck in a deep breath.

Apparently satisfied that the large canine standing on her deck meant her no harm, the cat walked to the front railing and lay in the sun.

Finally, broken from the cat's mesmerizing power, Bailey bounded over to Foxy. She play-bowed. She bumped her nose around the cat's gray and brown fur. She sniffed the stray's ears. And then with the family looking on in surprise, Bailey lay right next to the cat.

"I don't believe it," Jen whispered to her husband, who was looking very pleased with himself.

That spring day marked the beginning of a genuine friendship between the pampered pooch named Bailey and the ragtag stray named Foxy.

The two animals were as different as could be—from their size, to their species, to their temperaments. But somehow, someway, they became friends.

Friends who would call to each other from opposite sides of the back door.

Friends who would nuzzle each other and lie together in the sun.

Friends who would walk together in the evening with their human family—Bailey on a leash, Foxy running alongside in the drainage ditches.

And friends who were not the least bit concerned that people would say they weren't supposed to be.

Just two friends willing to take the time to get to know each other.

PAWS & PONDER...

Bailey and Foxy could not have been more different, and yet their differences are what made their friendship so special. In a world full of divisions—political, socio-economic, spiritual—it is easy to forget that God is the maker of us all. What differences are hard for you to see past in others? How do you think God wants his children to respond to those who are different?

Paws & Pray

Lord God, you made the world and filled it with people who are different from me in countless ways. God, help me to see others as you see them—fearfully and wonderfully created in your image. And when I become shortsighted and start to focus on the differences, convict me and remind me that you are God of us all.

85

TAKING TIME TO SEE

As water reflects the face, so one's life reflects the heart.

PROVERBS 27:19, NIV

MORGAN, A LARGE MALE PIT BULL MIX, might not fit most people's idea of a therapy dog. But just a few minutes with the stocky, gentle giant, and it is clear he is doing exactly what he was born to do.

It wasn't immediately apparent to April, a veterinarian who had been asked to volunteer with a pit bull rescue organization. Even she had been nervous the first time she met Morgan and the other pit bulls at the facility. She had fully anticipated encountering a bunch of mean, snarling dogs who would rather bite her than play with her.

But she could not have been more wrong.

What she had discovered instead were a bunch of loving dogs who simply needed a second chance and a good home. So she hadn't hesitated when they asked her to foster an injured bully mix named Morgan.

In her home, Morgan bonded strongly with April's German shepherd, Briley, a dog who had recently become certified as a therapy dog.

It wasn't long before April, her husband, Ben, and their sons, Cullen and Sutter, decided to give Morgan a forever home with them.

As April continued to get to know Morgan, she noticed the dog possessed an unusually gentle and patient temperament—qualities she knew would make him a great therapy dog.

But she also knew that pit bulls often got a bad rap and she wondered if Morgan would be accepted as a therapy dog.

What if the people he was there to comfort were too afraid to work with him?

After a few weeks of indecision over whether or not Morgan should become a therapy dog, April enrolled him in certification classes. And as she suspected, he was a natural, even graduating at the top of his canine class.

However, the real test came the first time Morgan went into a school to work with a group of children who were participating in a program designed to increase empathy and compassion.

Would the children be scared of him? Intimidated by his size and appearance?

They were.

Instead of eagerly approaching Morgan, they kept their distance and stared at him warily.

But April seized the opportunity to use their fear as the starting point to help them grasp a powerful lesson.

She asked the children to sit still and simply watch Morgan for a few minutes.

"Really look at him," she encouraged. "Not his size, or the shape of his head, or what color he is. Look at him—at what he is doing and how he is acting. Pay attention as he walks around the room—I promise he won't hurt you. Just watch him. And then in a few minutes I want you to tell me what you see."

The children complied for a few moments, staring intently at the dog.

Morgan slowly walked from child to child, sniffing their legs and nuzzling their hands.

A girl couldn't keep from giggling when Morgan sat on her foot.

A boy lowered his arm, wiggling his fingers in an attempt to lure Morgan over. When Morgan obliged, the boy gave him a vigorous head scratch.

After a few minutes April asked the group, "So what did you see? What do you think of Morgan?"

"He's really nice," the boy who was still scratching Morgan's head replied.

"He's funny," said the girl whose foot had been a temporary resting place for the dog.

Other voices chimed in. "He's gentle." "He's friendly." "I think he wants to be our friend."

April's heart swelled at their words. "Is he different from what you thought at first?" she asked.

Everyone nodded.

The children got on the floor and made a circle around Morgan, who was lying in the middle of the group. Each child put a hand on his large body, and April prompted them to talk about the danger of judging others based on their appearance or on the opinions of others. They discussed the importance of taking time to really see someone—to look past the outside things and see the person's heart.

Since that first classroom experience, Morgan has become an ambassador for his breed—a beautiful representation of a dog who overcame great difficulties and who now uses his gifts to spread joy and hope wherever he goes. April and Morgan are showing that dogs and humans come in all colors, shapes, and sizes and yet still can be wonderful friends.

PAWS & PONDER...

Have you ever been judged unfairly based on a physical attribute or undeserved reputation? How did it feel? Have you ever judged another person that way? What are some practical ways you can be more purposeful in how you see others? According to this proverb, a person's life reflects his or her heart. Ask God to show you what your life reveals about your heart. Confess those areas that do not align with God's own heart so that your heart might reflect his own.

Paws & Pray

Examine my heart, Lord. Reveal any unconfessed sin and prejudice I am harboring inside. Bring to the surface any thoughts of self-importance and unkindness. I desire a clean heart, Lord, so that I can reflect your beautiful face and your unfathomable love.

If you lie down, you will not be afraid;

when you lie down, your sleep will be sweet.

PROVERBS 3:24, ESV

86

A SECRET MELODY

No one who gossips can be trusted with a secret,
but you can put confidence in someone who is trustworthy.

PROVERBS 11:13, GNT

THE MOMENT KELLY SAW her eleven-year-old daughter Mia, she knew something was wrong. Her normally happy-go-lucky girl trudged through the pick-up line with drooped shoulders and downcast eyes. When she got into the car, Mia silently buckled her seat belt, folded her arms tightly around her middle, and let her head drop forward in defeat.

Mia's posture reminded Kelly why no amount of money would ever entice her to relive the middle-school years.

Change, she thought. *So many changes happen all at once.* As if changing classes, changing bodies, and changing hormones weren't enough to make even the happiest of children grumpy, the stress of changing friendships and learning (often the hard way) whom you can count on was enough to make every kid wish they could fast-forward through middle school.

So far, the most painful lesson for Mia was finding someone she could trust.

When Mia began to cry in the car, the story came out. Thinking her sixth-grade secrets—her crush on a classmate and her dream of being a princess at Disney World—were safe with the friends she had trusted since third grade, she had shared them. Her so-called friends had blabbed her confidences to the entire lunch table.

"I will never trust anyone again!" she vowed as they arrived home.

Inside the house, Melody, their four-year-old Golden-collie mix came bounding toward them. Mia dropped her backpack on the floor and ran into the family room. Kelly knelt down to pet Melody.

"I think someone needs a friend, Mellie," Kelly whispered.

Melody followed Kelly into the family room where Mia was lying face down on the sofa, a pillow over her head. Kelly sat down beside her daughter and began to rub her back. Melody put her head right beside Mia's. Her black nose pressed against Mia's wet cheek, and she began to lick the salty tears.

A small hand moved and gently touched Melody's side.

Kelly smiled.

"You know," Kelly said, "Melody is really good at keeping secrets."

Mia gave a muffled response. "That's because she can't talk."

"Exactly," Kelly said. "That's what makes her such an excellent secret keeper. After all, she's never told you any of my secrets, has she?"

Mia slipped the pillow under her head and turned over to look at her mother, switching hands to keep petting Melody.

"You tell Melody secrets?" Mia asked incredulously. "But you're a married grown-up! You don't have any secrets."

Kelly nearly choked on a laugh.

"Sure I do," she said. "Big ones too."

"Like what?" Mia asked skeptically.

Kelly hesitated before answering, lost in her own thoughts. *It's true. There are some things that I have never shared with anyone except Melody— and God.*

"Well, one secret I've told Melody that I'll share with you—because I know I can trust you—is that I'm scared of talking in front of people."

Mia sat up.

"But you talk in front of people all the time. It's part of your job."

Kelly grinned. "I know, but the truth is, I'm terrified every time I do it."

"Mama, can you tell me another one of your secrets?"

Kelly thought for a minute. "Want to know my biggest secret?"

Mia nodded.

"Deep down in my heart, I still feel like I'm in middle school and worried about what everyone thinks of me."

Mia laughed. "For real?"

"For real," Kelly admitted.

Mia scooted closer to Melody. "And Mellie helps you? Like when you talk to her?"

It was Kelly's turn to nod. "She sure does. Mellie always listens, even to my silliest fears and secrets. And I never ever have to worry about her laughing at me or telling anybody what I said. She really is man's—or rather, woman's—best friend."

Mia slid onto the floor next to Melody. "Do you mind if I talk to Melody for a little bit?"

Kelly kissed the top of Mia's head. "I don't mind at all. I'll leave the two of you alone." But just before leaving the room, Kelly turned around and looked lovingly at her daughter.

"Just remember. I'm pretty good at keeping secrets too."

A bright smile lit up Mia's face. "I know, Mama."

"Thank you, God," Kelly prayed out loud as she walked into the kitchen to start dinner. "Between you and Melody, I think we all just might survive the middle-school years."

PAWS & PONDER . . .

Have you ever been betrayed by someone you thought you could trust? Did it affect your willingness to trust others? Do you have a trusted confidant? Are you a confidant for someone else? Why is trust so important in relationships?

Paws & Pray

Father, no one is more trustworthy than you. Thank you for the dear friends and animals you've given me who remind me I can trust you—at all times. Help me to be a treasured and trustworthy friend to others.

87

CODY ON THE GO

Whoever gives heed to instruction prospers,
and blessed is the one who trusts in the LORD.

PROVERBS 16:20, NIV

MELISSA'S PHONE BUZZED IN HER POCKET.

"Running ten minutes late," the text from her neighbor Tish read. "Sorry."

Melissa slipped the phone back into her pocket and looked at her silver Lab's expectant expression.

"Sorry, Cody," she said, adjusting the leash that had gotten stuck under his back leg, "Gizmo's running a little late for our walk."

Cody, anxious to get moving, pulled on the leash.

"Okay, boy, I hear ya," she said. "We can walk for a bit while we wait for them."

Normally, Melissa and Tish kept a quick walking pace in the morning in order to get their active dogs as tired as possible before leaving them for the day. However, as Melissa waited for her friend and neighbor of seven years, she allowed Cody to set the pace. Melissa held the leash loosely in her hand and simply followed where he led. Cody was clearly thrilled with his freedom and investigated everything in sight. He sniffed bushes, he wandered into a clearing overlooking the creek that ran under the road. He discovered a turtle and attempted to play with it—until the odd-looking beast with the long leathery neck poked its head out of its shell.

Cody yelped in terror.

Melissa chuckled as she pulled him to safety on the other side of the road.

Cody recovered quickly from his fright and resumed his leisurely walk-and-sniff. Melissa enjoyed watching him explore. She laughed at his escapades and smiled at his discoveries. She even snapped a picture of Cody creeping back toward the turtle near the creek. But when the turtle's head emerged from its shell again, Cody dashed back to the road.

"No, Cody!" Melissa shouted, tightening up on the leash and pulling him back just as a car went by.

After redirecting him to another open area, Melissa again relaxed her hold on the leash.

Once again free to explore, Cody sniffed dandelions and pawed at a rock. But as he headed for a mud puddle, Melissa gave a quick tug on his leash.

"No, Cody!" she commanded.

The dog looked at her, then strained against the leash, wanting desperately to get to the enticing mud. Knowing how much he hated baths, Melissa pulled him back.

"Trust me, Codes," she said, urging him back to her side. "You aren't gonna like where that mud leads."

She clicked her tongue and started dragging an insistent and disgruntled Cody back toward Gizmo's house. He barked his displeasure and he thrashed his head, trying to break free. Melissa was grateful for the new, more secure harness he now wore. Several weeks earlier he had wiggled out of the collar and chased a squirrel for half a block. Cody was lovable and playful, but he was also headstrong and opinionated.

"Come on, boy," Melissa panted. "Let's go find Gizmo."

Cody stopped mid-tug. The mud was immediately forgotten when Cody heard the name Gizmo, and he eagerly pulled Melissa toward his beagle friend's house.

As Melissa followed her spirited dog, she realized how much she was just like her dog. God gave her so much freedom. And surely he delighted in watching her experience every blessing he had given her.

Yet how many times had she pulled against his plans for her? How much trouble could she have avoided if she had heeded his warning? And how many messes did she create by insisting on going her own way?

She drew Cody to her side, kneeling to hug him close.

Whispering a prayer of repentance and thanksgiving, Melissa planted a kiss on Cody's head.

A slobbery kiss across her face ended her prayer. As she stood, she caught a glimpse of Gizmo and Tish heading their way.

"I see Gizmo!" she told her panting Lab.

And with those words Cody was off—with Melissa sprinting right behind.

PAWS & PONDER...

We have great freedom in Christ, and yet, in his love, he has set boundaries for us—to protect us and spare us from unnecessary pain. How often do you try to push past divine boundaries, insisting you know better? What mud puddle are you heading toward today? What might happen if you insist on going your own way? Are you willing to trust God and walk back to him?

Paws & Pray

Lord, so often I think I know better than you. I strive to go my own way and pull away from you. Father, forgive me and draw me back to you. Help me to trust your plan more than my own. And give me courage to walk away from the mud puddles of this life and walk on clear paths with you.

88

𝒜N ◎PEN 𝒟OOR

Listen to advice and accept instruction,
that you may gain wisdom in the future.

PROVERBS 19:20, ESV

THE THEME SONG TO *MY LITTLE PONY* grated on Lindsey's nerves as she stared at her laptop's blank screen. She typed five words. Deleted them. Typed four more . . .

"My little pony, my little pony . . ."

"Harper!" she yelled to her seven-year-old daughter who was home sick with a fever. "Please turn that down! Mommy has to work."

The volume was lowered a few decibels. Lindsey managed to type six sentences on her proposal before being interrupted once again—this time by Beau, their sixty-pound boxer whom Lindsey had forgotten to feed that morning.

"Sorry, bud," she apologized, walking into the kitchen. Lindsey scooped an extra large portion of kibble into his bowl. "Forgive me?"

She took her dog's loud, spittle-flying chomping as a yes.

With Beau happily eating and Harper situated on the sofa, Lindsey sat back down to continue working. She rubbed her neck and pressed her fingers into her temple. She had to get her proposal finished, respond to more emails than she cared to think about, and be in the car line by three o'clock to get her ten-year-old son.

She took a deep breath. "I can do this," she assured herself.

"My little pony . . ." Another episode already?

Lindsey looked up at the ceiling, her confidence waning. Then

Harper began coughing. *Poor baby.* Lindsey wanted to snuggle with her sick girl on the sofa, but she had a deadline. She had to work.

Instead of yelling at Harper to turn the volume down even more, Lindsey closed the door between the dining room and the great room, where Harper was watching TV. Finally, the sound of the ponies was at a tolerable level.

Lindsay again began to type. The words flowed easily.

Scratch, scratch, scratch.

Beau was digging at the tile on the other side of the swinging door.

"Beau, come around the other way," Lindsey instructed, her fingers beating a staccato rhythm on her laptop.

The dog whined before firing off three rapid-fire yelps.

Lindsey dropped her head in her hands. "Beau, come!"

Scratch, scratch, scratch.

"Beau, there's an open doorway six feet away from you." Lindsey raised her voice in exasperation. "Come!"

The boxer used both doors regularly, but apparently finding one of the doors closed caused him to panic and be confused.

Beau was fixated on the closed door, refusing to even consider another possibility. Instead, he whined, pawed at the door, and scratched at the tile, before eventually dropping to the floor with a loud sigh—resigned to wait for Lindsey.

Lindsey shook her head at her dog's stubborn cluelessness.

Yet at the same moment she felt God whisper to her soul: *My love, aren't you doing the same thing?*

Her heart beat wildly with an awareness her mind had yet to process. Lindsey had been beating her head on the door of "I-can-do-it-all-myself" for so long that she couldn't even recognize any other open doors.

She smiled as the sound of talking ponies wafted under the door. Yes, she had a deadline. But she also had a sick little girl who needed her.

Lindsey pulled the door open, surprising Beau in mid-jump. Two big paws landed on her waist.

"Come on, boy," Lindsey said and chuckled, gently pushing the dog's chest to get him back on all four legs. "Let's go watch some ponies with our girl."

Harper's eyes widened as Lindsey snuggled in beside her. She smiled, revealing two recently lost teeth.

"Mama, what about your work?" she asked, her last word swallowed up in a dry, hacking cough.

Lindsey kissed the top of her daughter's head. "I'll get it done in a little while—after I snuggle with my favorite girl for a bit." She pulled Harper into an embrace. Glancing at Beau she added, "I'm gonna walk through a different door today, baby girl."

PAWS & PONDER...

Sometimes God asks us to wait for him to open a door, while other times he opens a different door for us. Have you been desperate to go through a door that simply refuses to open? Will you ask God for the discernment to know when to wait for him to open a door and when to look for an alternate path?

Paws & Pray

Lord, so often I try to beat a door down, convinced it is the only way to reach a plan you have for me. Would you help me identify which doors you want me to walk through and which ones to leave closed? Let me only walk through the doors you open for me. And Father, if I need to wait, give me patience to accept the delay.

Look straight ahead, and fix your
eyes on what lies before you.

PROVERBS 4:25

89

ℒEARNING ℱO ℱRUST

Trust in the LORD with all your heart; do not depend

on your own understanding. Seek his will in all you do,

and he will show you which path to take.

PROVERBS 3:5-6

DEPUTY FIELD CROSS KNOWS that trust does not always come easily, that it is often built slowly and is the result of hard work, perseverance, and time.

And as a K9 officer with the bloodhound unit in Halifax County, Virginia, Deputy Cross also knows that trust can save your life.

Working with bloodhounds—whether searching for a missing person or hunting down a suspect—requires enormous trust between handler and dog.

When tracking a criminal through dense woods, handlers must know their dogs' body languages. The K9 officers must be able to tell instantly if their dogs' sudden wagging tails or raised heads are a signal that a suspect is nearby or simply a reaction to another animal's scent. They also need to know what distracts their dogs, how their dogs react to various stimuli, and how best to keep their canine partners focused in potentially dangerous situations.

Deputy Cross had worked so long and spent so much time with his K9 partner, Sidney, that the two often functioned as one. Their bond was so strong that Deputy Cross could tell if Sidney was closing in on a suspect just by a slight change in the tension of the leash.

Of course, Sidney's single-mindedness when he was on the job made it pretty easy for Deputy Cross to trust the bloodhound. It seemed Sidney's only objective in life was to find what he was told to find. He always stayed on task.

Deputy Cross's confidence in his K9 partner's skills enabled them to do their jobs well and save countless lives in the process.

And it was also that trust that made saying goodbye extremely difficult.

When Sidney suffered congestive heart failure two days before Christmas, Deputy Cross stayed by the regal bloodhound's side until the end. Brokenhearted yet grateful to have worked with Sidney, Deputy Cross began the search for a new partner.

Yet he feared he would never again find a dog as trustworthy as Sidney.

He contacted the Find M' Friends bloodhound training team in Citrus County, Florida, a nonprofit organization that acquires and trains bloodhounds for search and rescue and then gifts them to law enforcement. The organization was delighted to present year-old Gus to Deputy Cross and the Halifax County bloodhound unit.

Two months after losing Sidney, Deputy Cross began working with Gus.

Gus came well-trained in scent discrimination, and Deputy Cross was confident Gus would become a capable and excellent partner. And yet, he also realized it was going to take time to trust Gus as much as he had trusted Sidney. The two of them needed to learn each other's cues, mannerisms, and signals. Deputy Cross and Gus had to learn how to communicate effectively with each other, how to fight distractions, and how to prepare for the unknown. Bonding wouldn't happen overnight. It would take time to get to know each other, time that would result in Deputy Cross being able to trust Gus to lead and guide him with his nose, in hopes of saving someone's life.

PAWS & PONDER...

Trust. What do you think of when you hear that word? Does trusting others come easily to you? What about trusting God? Why is spending time with God necessary in order for you to trust him to lead?

Paws & Pray

God, you are far more trustworthy than I am. And yet so often I don't trust you. Lord, stir my heart to desire you more by spending time with you through your Word, in prayer, and in quiet moments. As my trust grows, help me follow where you lead.

90

TRYING TO HOLD IT
ALL TOGETHER

Hatred stirs up strife, but love covers all offenses.

PROVERBS 10:12, ESV

SHARON WAS BARELY HOLDING IT TOGETHER. Her fingers tingled and her mind was fuzzy. She had no idea she was breathing too fast. All she knew was a snowstorm was headed their way, her newborn son had given up sleeping, and her husband's plane was due to land in an hour. Oh, and there was no food in the house.

Trying to clear her throat from whatever felt lodged in it, Sharon fought against her panic.

The Weather Channel droned on the television in the background, taunting her for her lack of preparations. But who could prepare for anything with an infant who refused to sleep!

And why did her husband have to be out of town on a business trip this week?

Sure, his boss had told him he had to go, but one look around the messy house and at her reflection in the hallway mirror and she suspected that he had been relieved to leave for a few days. *I wish I could spend a few nights by myself at a hotel,* she thought, then immediately felt guilty for wanting to be away from her baby.

All she had ever wanted was to be a mom. But she had no idea it would be so hard. Or involve such little sleep.

Buster, their yellow Lab, came bounding up to Sharon, clearly wanting to play.

"No, Buster," she shouted, startling her son who had just dozed off in the swing.

She couldn't hold back a fresh round of tears. It all felt like too much.

Buster dropped his ball at Sharon's feet, bumped his head against her leg, and barked expectantly.

Sharon screamed at Buster as she shoved him away. She picked up his slobbery ball and threw it as hard as she could, knocking over a lamp.

The dog backed away. The baby started to cry. And Sharon sank to the kitchen floor and wept.

She felt like a horrible mom, a horrible wife, a horrible snowstorm-ready person, and now a horrible dog owner.

As she sat with her hands covering her eyes, her son's cries began to subside. Sharon peeked through two fingers.

Buster was standing by the infant swing. The baby's eyes were fixed on the dog. Buster turned his head toward Sharon.

"Oh, Buster," she sobbed. "I am so sorry."

Her Lab, who didn't know the meaning of holding a grudge, walked over to Sharon and put his head on her shoulder.

Sharon held on to the strong dog as she let every fear and anxiety rise to the surface. Buster never moved and remained by her side until every tear was spilled.

With her son sound asleep in the swing, Sharon put on her coat and took Buster outside to play catch.

Minutes later her husband texted to say his plane had landed, and he was going to stop by the store on his way home.

Sharon's anxiety immediately began to dissipate when she read those words.

This time when Buster dropped his ball at her feet, Sharon kissed his head before tossing the toy.

"My steady, loving, forgiving, and slobbery Buster," she cooed. "What would I do without you?"

PAWS & PONDER...

Why do you think fear and anxiety cause a person to act out in anger and hate? Why can responding in love sometimes feel so difficult? Are you facing a difficult situation today? Ask God to show you how to respond in love.

Paws & Pray

Lord, you are love. Whenever I want to react angrily, please help me to stop and think before I say or do anything. Then give me the words to respond to others in love—in person, on the phone, on social media. Father, I need your discernment to know how to respond lovingly to difficult situations that arise, even today.

91

TRAINING CASH

Hold on to instruction, do not let it go;

guard it well, for it is your life.

PROVERBS 4:13, NIV

AMY DIDN'T KNOW WHO WAS MORE anxious on the first night of puppy class—Cash, her black Labrador retriever, or herself. She was convinced that she would be hopeless as a trainer, and she feared they would be the first duo to flunk out of puppy school on the first night! Cash was sweet as could be, but he was a handful—a ball of kinetic energy and insatiable hunger contained in a black fur coat.

Amy stole a glance around the large training room and felt better. *Everyone looks as scared as me.* They were all struggling to keep their dogs from jumping, barking, and pulling at their leashes.

When the trainer told the class that their first objective was simply to follow their dogs around the arena to allow them a few minutes to get comfortable with their surroundings, Amy breathed a sigh of relief. She definitely could walk behind Cash without too much trouble.

The night progressed fairly smoothly until Cash decided to relieve himself in the middle of a heeling exercise. Amy was embarrassed, especially when most of the other people in the class started to laugh.

And yet, remarkably, Cash learned to heel, sit, and stay by the end of the night.

Each week, the trainer reviewed the previous week's commands, introduced a new command, encouraged the handlers to use longer leashes, and asked them to keep their dogs in longer sit-stays. Then the instructor threw toys into the ring and made loud noises to distract the canines while they were going through their drills. Cash proved to be a natural learner, and Amy was amazed by how quickly he was able to perfect a new skill. She appreciated the structured training methods that she could easily replicate between classes with Cash. The two of them practiced diligently at home.

One Saturday, Amy and Cash were practicing a down-stay in the front yard. Amy was using a fifteen-foot leash (compared to the usual six-foot leash), and Cash was doing a great job until . . . something in the distance caught his attention and he broke the down-stay so unexpectedly that the end of the leash slipped from Amy's hand.

When Cash realized he was untethered, he leapt with glee and bolted.

Panic shot through Amy's limbs like electric shocks as she imagined the dangers Cash might encounter on his joy-run through the neighborhood.

But then Amy remembered their training. *Maybe it will work?*

"Cash!" she hollered tentatively, then more forcefully as the trainer had instructed. "Cash, *come!*"

And to Amy's astonishment, he did.

"Good boy, good boy!" she praised him, as the exuberant puppy ran into her arms.

Amy gave him treat after treat, which he happily gobbled. Then she gave him a thorough belly rub before picking up his leash and offering a prayer of thanksgiving. With the leash wrapped tightly around her wrist, Amy and Cash continued practicing down-stays.

There's a possibility Cash might run away again, Amy thought. *But thankfully, he responds to my voice.* She took comfort in that fact, grateful for the hours of training she and Cash had spent together.

PAWS & PONDER . . .

Cash's training took time. He had to learn to listen and respond to Amy's voice. Are you spending time with God? How might you train yourself to better hear his voice and then respond accordingly?

Paws & Pray

Father, I know that your instructions for my life are found in your Word. Help me to set aside time each day to read and meditate on it. For your Word is life-giving, and your voice offers truth. Grant me the self-control I need to ignore the voices of distraction that drive me off your path. Help me to recognize your voice and be willing to quickly respond to it when you speak.

92

ƑINDING ƑORREST

If you become wise, you will be the one to benefit.
If you scorn wisdom, you will be the one to suffer.

PROVERBS 9:12

IT WAS GETTING CLOSE TO CHRISTMAS, and the Colins family hadn't seen their cat, Forrest, in days. Since finding the tan, gray, and black tabby two years ago living in the woods behind their house, he had shown up on the back deck for dinner every day.

Forrest was an affectionate cat who let his adopted family love him back. He regularly left thank-you "gifts" at the back door—sometimes dead squirrels that were half his size.

At first, the family didn't worry too much about Forrest's absence. They figured their tough cat could take care of himself. But as one day turned into two and two into three without any sign of him, they began to worry.

On Christmas night, they heard a louder than normal meow coming from the back deck. When twenty-year-old John opened the back door, he found Forrest standing there, shaking and wide-eyed. Then John noticed Forrest's fur was matted with blood. He saw the wound on the cat's neck.

"Quick! Forrest is hurt!"

John carefully picked up the cat. John's mom, Deb, was already in the garage making a bed for Forrest out of a discarded box that hours earlier had contained a beanbag chair. She laid the cardboard container on its side and filled it with a flannel sheet and an old comforter. John gingerly laid Forrest inside.

"Oh, he smells awful," Deb said, sighing. "What on earth happened to him?"

Addie, John's sixteen-year-old sister, walked into the garage carrying a handful of turkey and a bowl of milk. Addie hand-fed Forrest, who gulped everything down. "He probably hasn't eaten for days," Addie said.

Deb called the emergency vet and got instructions for keeping Forrest as comfortable as possible. After a family discussion, they agreed it would be less stressful to keep Forrest at home and have a mobile vet come to them.

"Yes, Forrest was definitely attacked by an animal," the vet concluded. "It could have been a fox or a dog, or possibly a raccoon."

After confirming that Forrest was up to date on his rabies shots, the vet cleaned the wound and gave Forrest a shot of antibiotics.

"Call me if there are any problems," the vet said.

For the next week, Forrest stayed in the garage, feasting on leftover turkey, using a litter box, and lapping up lots of extra attention. Eventually, the wound healed, and Forrest was ready to return to his outdoor life.

At first he seemed thrilled to be back outside as he ran straight to the edge of the woods.

John watched as Forrest crept toward a robin in the underbrush and silently rejoiced when the bird flew away before Forrest got too close.

Before long, Forrest was on the deck, napping in his favorite spot.

But as the sun disappeared below the horizon, Forrest began yowling and scratching at the back door. The moment Deb opened the door, Forrest ran inside and straight to the door leading into the garage.

"A little scared to be out there tonight, huh, bud? You'll be safe here," Deb said, opening the door into the garage. Forrest ran straight to his king-size bed and snuggled in for the night.

The Colins family will never know what happened to their cat during the few days before Christmas, but it seems Forrest has not forgotten. He now sleeps in the family's garage every night.

"You think Forrest knows that whatever hurt him is still out there?" Addie asked John.

John smiled. "Well, it's either that or he discovered the comfort of a soft bed and a tasty meal of turkey! Either way, he's a pretty smart cat."

PAWS & PONDER . . .

Have you ever suffered because you acted foolishly? Can you think of a specific benefit you received when you acted wiser? Why is it often hard to change our behavior, even though we know we should?

Paws & Pray

Father, thank you for supplying all my needs from your abundant resources. You are always teaching me to be wise in everything I do. Please help me not just to fill my mind with knowledge, but to be willing to use that knowledge sensibly. When I start to go off course and wander into danger, please draw me back to you. Help me to be an example to others.

When people's lives please the Lᴏʀᴅ, even their
enemies are at peace with them.

PROVERBS 16:7

93

𝒜 GOOD 𝓂OVE

Unrelenting disappointment leaves you heartsick,

but a sudden good break can turn life around.

PROVERBS 13:12, MSG

NOTHING BROUGHT A SMILE to Crystal Kranz's face more than her spunky twelve-pound dog Alfie, a chihuahua-yorkie mix. The two had been inseparable for ten years and during that time, Alfie had honed a particular outdoor skill.

Chasing rabbits.

It wasn't unusual or unexpected. Many dogs chased rabbits, birds, squirrels—anything that moved. But over time Crystal realized Alfie's true motive. He wasn't hunting rabbits; he just wanted to play with the fluffy animals that were the same size as he was! He wanted to be friends.

When Alfie spotted his would-be pals through the glass patio door, he'd prance and wag his tail so fast, Crystal half expected him to start levitating. When she would finally fetch Alfie's leash, he would let out a little whine of anticipation. The game was on.

"Okay, Alfie," Crystal said, clicking a leash to his collar and slowly sliding the patio door open.

She knew from experience how Alfie's enthusiasm could get the best of him if he wasn't given parameters. If he had his way, Alfie would romp with rabbits near and far. A twenty-five-foot lead gave him access to the entire backyard, but still kept him contained.

Crystal remembered when Alfie had almost succeeded in his quest. He was sunbathing on the patio and spotted a young rabbit nibbling on the grass near the steps. Alfie darted across the deck, down the stairs, stumbled on the last step, and somersaulted over the visitor, who was too stunned to move. The two looked at each other as if to say, *Now what?* The rabbit made a mad dash across the lawn and disappeared through an opening in the fence. Alfie's attempt at friendship was foiled again.

Months went by and Crystal's life circumstances changed. Her hope for a lifetime of fulfilled dreams had crumbled when her eight-year marriage ended. It made her heartsick. Suddenly, things in the house were packed in boxes, including Alfie's toys, bed, blankets, and dishes. The house got emptier and emptier. Finally, when Crystal put Alfie in the car, she explained that they were moving.

The new house was smaller, with no deck for sunbathing or large backyard to explore.

But Crystal was there.

The two of them began venturing out, meeting new neighbors with their dogs.

On a walk a week later, Crystal stopped to chat with another new neighbor. The woman held a leash in her hand and on the other end . . . Alfie couldn't believe his eyes. There was a rabbit standing right next to him! The rabbit stretched up on his hind legs and sniffed Alfie. This seemed too good to be true!

"This is Peanut," the woman said. "He loves going for walks."

Even more amazing, Peanut lived next door!

It wasn't long before the two best friends began having regular play-dates inside and outside. They shared toys and cuddled together. Alfie's dream had been fulfilled, even better than he imagined. And Crystal? Her new dream was a work in process, but she was certain God would provide the best plan going forward.

PAWS & PONDER . . .

What plans or dreams have you had to surrender? What life goals haven't turned out the way you had imagined they would? Where did you find hope? What or who has been your constant? Remember that God has promised never to leave you or forsake you.

———————————— ✹ ————————————

Paws & Pray

Father, in a world that can bring disappointment and hurt, you are my constant hope. Help me to trust in you and hold fast to you through the ups and downs I face. When my confidence falters, enable me to believe that you have the best plans for my life.

94

A FRIEND FOR TREVOR

One who has unreliable friends soon comes to ruin,

but there is a friend who sticks closer than a brother.

PROVERBS 18:24, NIV

THE BOY SAT BY HIMSELF eyeing the camp activities going on around him. His arms were tightly folded, and a scowl was etched on his face. Nothing about his appearance was inviting. However, the boy's demeanor did nothing to dissuade Sandee's dog, Tesla, from approaching him.

Sandee and her certified therapy dog had recently arrived at a summer camp held for more than one hundred children in foster care. They were one of three therapy dog teams attending the weeklong camp. Sandee looked forward to the annual camp each year and was delighted that volunteers with the Divine Dogs ministry she had started at her church were able to be a part of the special week.

The Divine Dogs teams arrived the second day of camp. They were greeted with loud cheers and giggles, which had warmed Sandee's heart. Yet the other children's exuberance made her notice the boy sitting by himself. His demeanor was in stark contrast to the laughing children huddled around Tesla and the other dogs.

As the initial excitement ebbed, the counselors directed the children toward an open field where they had set up all sorts of games. Sandee had been planning to use the time to get herself and Tesla situated in their cabin. However, Tesla had other plans.

The Golden retriever began walking toward the boy still sitting on the curb in front of the welcome center. The boy cast a quick glance her way, before turning his body from her. Sandee could almost feel his hostility and pain.

"Hi," she said, her voice upbeat and friendly. "I'm Sandee and this is Tesla. I think she would like to say hi to you. Is that okay?"

Silence. A slight shrug of the shoulders.

Sandee nodded to Tesla, an unspoken signal that she may say hello.

"This is Tesla's third year at camp. She really loves it. Have you been here before?"

Silence.

Tesla placed her head on the boy's knees. After several seconds he touched her forehead with one finger.

He shook his head.

"Oh, so it's your first time," Sandee concluded from the headshake. "Well, you've already made one friend. Tesla sure does like you!"

The boy started stroking Tesla's back. She sat down in front of him and offered her paw.

A smile lit up the boy's face as he shook her paw.

"What's your name?" Sandee asked. "I know Tesla would like to know her new friend's name."

The boy looked at Tesla when he spoke. "My name is Trevor."

"Well, Trevor, it is nice to meet you. I'm glad you're here so Tesla can have such a good friend." An idea formed in Sandee's mind. "I actually need to get settled into my cabin. Would you like to walk Tesla over there with me?"

Sandee was surprised when Trevor agreed. He held Tesla's leash as they walked to the cabin.

Over the next week, Trevor and Tesla were rarely apart. The boy walked her twice a day, played fetch with her in the field, and even demonstrated some of Tesla's tricks to the other kids. But what amazed Sandee the most was that Tesla often sought out Trevor. She searched for him in a group, turned when she heard his voice, or patiently waited for him to finish an activity. Tesla had never been so attuned to one child before.

"Will Tesla be here next year?" Trevor asked Sandee on the last night of camp.

Sandee assured him Tesla would be returning. Trevor hugged the dog lying in his lap, then looked up at Sandee.

"Ms. Sandee, do you think she will remember me?" the boy asked quietly, the vulnerability in his eyes bringing tears to Sandee's own.

"Oh, Trevor, I know she will remember you. You are her friend, and Tesla never ever forgets her friends."

"I love you, Tesla," Trevor whispered. "Thank you for being my friend."

PAWS & PONDER...

What is the difference between an unreliable and a reliable friend? Who are your most reliable friends? In what ways have they shown you their reliability? Take a moment today and thank them for being such good friends.

Paws & Pray

Lord, thank you for the friends you have given me, especially those I know I can always count on. Help me to be a reliable, loyal friend to others and to always point each one of them to you—the most loyal and loving friend of all.

95

THE STENCH OF REJECTION

The prudent sees danger and hides himself,

but the simple go on and suffer for it.

PROVERBS 27:12, ESV

"**SMOKEY!** No!" Tara yelled frantically, trying to rein in the retractable leash. "Leave it. Stop. Sit. Stay. Come!"

Her dog ignored the staccato commands and forged ahead toward his goal—a black and white animal nosing around some bushes. Even though it was dark, Tara could make out the telltale stripe. But her attempts at reeling in her strong hound mix were useless. He was straining against the leash like a sled dog on track to win the Iditarod single handedly.

"The skunk is not your friend!" Tara explained. "He doesn't want to have anything to do with you. He would rather spray than play."

It wasn't like Smokey hadn't been down this odorous road before. He had been sprayed three times in the past year. Each time, Tara was certain he had learned his lesson.

Normally, she loved Smokey's tenacity. After all, it was his tenacity that saved his life after being so horribly abused as a puppy. His will to live and determination to survive were evident the first time Tara met him at the animal shelter and fell instantly in love with him. And yet, right now, she really wished he would dial his determination down a few notches.

"Smokey, let me tell you again. That skunk does not want to be your friend. He hasn't wanted to be a friend all year. Come on, let's get . . ." Too late. The skunk suddenly stopped, lifted its tail, and took aim.

Smokey jumped back. He sneezed and shook his head. Then he ran back to Tara, dejected and confused. His expression broke her heart, and the pungent smell wafting from him stung her eyes. Tara covered her nose and mouth and muffled, "Bath time for you, mister. Thankfully, I still have a full bottle of Skunk-Off shampoo at home."

Actually, she had three full bottles. After all, you can never have enough neutralizing shampoo when you live in an area where cranky skunks abound.

"Oh, buddy," she said, resisting the urge to pet her dog. "When are you gonna learn that Mr. Stink Spray will never be your playmate?"

Smokey cast a pitiful look toward the bushes where the skunk had disappeared. He then looked up at Tara.

"I know, I know. How humiliating, especially when your intentions were good and noble." She tugged on his leash. "Come on, let's go home and wash away the stench of rejection."

PAWS & PONDER...

There are times when temptation seems unavoidable—it just seems to come out of nowhere. But other times, like today's proverb describes, you see temptation coming and have a chance to get away. Can you recall a time when temptation suddenly appeared? What about a time when you clearly saw it coming? What temptations do you struggle with most? What are some safeguards you can put in place today to avoid the stench of sin?

Paws & Pray

Lord, thank you for always making a way for me either to stand against or run from temptation. Forgive me when I fail, when I pursue sin, knowing full well the consequences. Enable me to recognize temptation when it is coming my way. And give me the strength to run and hide. Help me to see you as bigger than any sin and any temptation. And help me to trust you far more than I trust myself.

96

SWEET PEA'S MITTEN

The greedy stir up conflict,

but those who trust in the LORD will prosper.

PROVERBS 28:25, NIV

CAN THIS WEEK PLEASE *go by a little faster?* Carolyn thought as she waited anxiously to bring her new kitten home.

After losing her beloved cat, Winnie, earlier that summer—and grieving more than she had thought possible—Carolyn was ready to bring a new companion into her life. She was delighted when she saw the kitten from the Paws Humane Society online. She just had to wait until the kitten she had named Sweet Pea turned eight weeks old.

In an attempt to keep herself busy while she waited, Carolyn got out needles and yarn and began knitting—something she enjoyed but hadn't done in quite a while. It didn't take her long to create cute toys in the shape of tiny multicolored mittens, made irresistible with catnip inside. She planned to put one in Sweet Pea's carrier for the ride home and keep the other for safekeeping.

Finally, the week was up. When Carolyn brought Sweet Pea home, the mitten was larger than the kitten's head. Sweet Pea would lie on the mitten like a pillow, cuddle it like a stuffed animal, and curl up on it like it was a tiny bed.

As Sweet Pea grew, she took her mitten everywhere. Wherever she was, mitten was there too. The mitten became her lovey, her comfort item, and her friend. She would cling to it when she was upset and bring it to Carolyn when Mommy was upset. In fact, it was so cherished that it started showing signs of wear and tear.

Carolyn tried switching it out for the identical match, but Sweet Pea rejected the imposter. After listening to her cat pitifully carry on for more than an hour, Carolyn made a few repairs to the original mitten and gave it back to Sweet Pea. Her cries became purrs as she nuzzled her treasure.

For three and a half years, as the well-loved mitten began to show its age, Carolyn tried unsuccessfully to swap it out with mitten #2, but Sweet Pea would have none of it.

There may be a time in the future when the old mitten will be too far gone. But not now. Her tiny mitten is enough for her.

Sweet Pea trusted Carolyn to take care of her, and she trusted her catnip mitten to comfort her.

Carolyn took this illustration of contentment to heart as she and Sweet Pea moved into their new home two years later. Every time Carolyn started looking for just one more item for the house, she would stop and smile, thinking of Sweet Pea's favorite mitten and questioning the necessity of another household purchase.

Thanks, Sweet Pea, for the reminder. I have everything I need, and it really is plenty.

PAWS & PONDER...

What do trusting in the Lord and being content have to do with prospering? In what ways do we prosper by trusting in the Lord? Conversely, what kind of conflict might we find ourselves in by being greedy or discontent?

Paws & Pray

God, I have everything I need in you. And yet I often want more and more material things in order to feel satisfied. Father, fill my heart with an awareness of your presence so that I will focus less on acquiring more things. Remind me of your sufficiency and love and how you provide good things for me. Help me to be grateful for everything you have given me and to be content.

Do not let wisdom and understanding
out of your sight.

PROVERBS 3:21, NIV

97

GYPSY'S TREASURES

Keep my words and treasure up my commandments with you.

PROVERBS 7:1, ESV

NICOLE SAT BACK ON HER KNEES to survey her work. Twenty bright orange marigolds now lined the walkway to her front door. As she patted the soil around the cheerfully colored plants, the corner of a foil wrapper caught her eye. She took her spade and unearthed a protein bar still in its wrapper.

Who would bury a protein bar? she pondered as she threw it in the garbage can.

A few days later her son Landon walked in the back door carrying a plastic bag containing the remnants of a loaf of bread.

"Uh, Mom?" he asked. "Why did you bury the bread?"

Landon had discovered the bag, half covered with dirt in their patchy side yard when he was mowing. He had also found an empty water bottle and some loose magazine pages.

Over the next few weeks, they discovered more and more buried items: plastic grocery bags, a banana peel, an old flip-flop, and a pair of gardening gloves—which Nicole hadn't seen in months.

Nicole's family had three dogs—two Yorkshire terriers and a chocolate Lab, Gypsy. Nicole immediately eliminated the Yorkies as suspects; they didn't even like the feel of grass on their paws. *Gypsy!*

And sure enough, the next day Nicole watched another caper unfold from start to finish. That afternoon she was throwing what was left of Landon's lunch into the trash, including an empty Gatorade bottle, when Gypsy ran through the doggie door. As she resumed other tasks, Nicole saw Gypsy sneak the bottle out of the garbage and run out the doggie door.

She then watched from the kitchen window as Gypsy frantically dug a hole near the deck and dropped her treasure inside. After pawing the dirt back over the bottle, Gypsy lay down several feet in front of her concealed plunder.

"You silly dog," Nicole said and chuckled, completely baffled by her dog's pirate-like behavior.

Nicole and her family tried to break Gypsy of her burying habit, but the dog was determined to keep a secret stash of miscellaneous household items and trash. As Gypsy got older, she even began burying things inside the house—under blankets, in piles of dirty laundry, or shoved under the sofa.

Over time Nicole realized the things Gypsy buried were items Nicole's family had touched, eaten, or used. Treats, toys, trash. If her humans had touched it, Gypsy wanted to keep it.

"You keep some funny treasures, Gypsy," Nicole said one night, rubbing the now white fur on her dog's muzzle. "But you gotta keep what's important close to you, huh?"

Nicole cast a glance at the coffee table that held a family photo and her well-worn Bible—the Bible she had treasured and held close for decades.

"Me too, baby girl," she said, warmth spreading through her heart. "Me too."

PAWS & PONDER...

Why is it important for us to keep and treasure God's Word? By keeping God's Word in our minds, we are able to treasure it in our hearts. What are some practical ways you can keep God's Word in your mind and in your heart this week? What is one verse you will commit to memory this month?

Paws & Pray

Father, thank you for the gift of your Word. When I read it, I believe you are personally speaking to me. Give me a passion and desire to keep your words in my mind and in my heart. God, help me treasure your words above all others.

98

$\mathcal{P}$RAYING $\mathcal{F}$OR $\mathcal{P}$IPPA

Anxiety weighs down the heart, but a kind word cheers it up.

PROVERBS 12:25, NIV

PATTI WAS ANXIOUS. *But probably not as anxious as Pippa will be when Terri and Joe leave,* she thought. Pippa, a Maltese mix, adored Patti's sister and brother-in-law. Whenever Joe traveled for work, Pippa would get so upset she would refuse to eat or go outside.

Now both of them were going on a mission trip. How would little Pippa react to both Joe *and* Terri leaving her for two weeks?

When Terri asked Patti if she could watch Pippa, she couldn't say no. Patti knew she needed to be there for the dog. And besides, Patti's son, Cal, loved Pippa and was looking forward to taking care of her.

So Patti agreed and began to pray for the dog.

Patti suspected that whenever Joe and Terri were gone, the little dog believed her dear ones were lost forever and she mourned that they would never return. Patti decided to ask God to turn the little dog's mourning into joyful dancing.

Patti was diligent in her prayers for Pippa and recruited Cal and her husband, Wendel, to pray too. Even before Terri and Joe left on their trip, Patti would go over and spend time with Pippa, assuring her about all the fun they would have together. Patti even spoke Bible verses over her.

"Psalm 30:11 says God can turn mourning into dancing, Pippa. So we trust him to cause your little heart to dance with joy even while Joe and Terri are gone."

Finally, the day of Terri and Joe's departure arrived—along with the real test of how Pippa would react.

Patti tried to walk in the house with great confidence when she went by to check on Pippa, claiming every promise she had prayed over the dog. And yet, the truth was, she was a little panicky.

Would God answer a prayer for a dog's mental health?

From the moment Cal opened the door, Pippa began jumping and whimpering in joy. She ran circles around Cal, Patti, and Wendel. Pippa grabbed her tennis ball and dropped it at Cal's feet, clearly wanting to play fetch.

After several minutes of play, Patti watched in awe as Pippa ran to her food and water bowl and looked at Patti as if to say, "I'm ready for dinner now." And when Pippa scampered out through her doggie door to take care of her business, Patti couldn't hold back a shout of delight.

Since that time, Pippa has never had any issues when Terri and Joe go abroad for mission trips, and Patti and her family are always overjoyed to take care of her.

Pippa's worry and sadness were no match for Patti's words of kindness and prayer. Nor were they any match for the God whose grace extends even to the animals his children love so much.

PAWS & PONDER . . .

What has you in knots today? Will you take some time to read the Bible and allow God's kind words to infuse your heart with joy? Can you remember a time when someone prayed for you and spoke kind words to you, and your burden was lightened? Will you pray and ask God to allow you to speak words of kindness and life to someone today?

Paws & Pray

Lord God, so often I am anxious about situations, big and small. I know that you ask me to bring all my cares to you. I believe you hear my requests; I have witnessed answers to prayer so many times. I bring everything to you, praising your name, my true source of joy and peace.

99

REMEMBER YOUR PACK

Know the state of your flocks, and put your
heart into caring for your herds.

PROVERBS 27:23

WITH HER HEAD HIGH and tail swaying, Penny, a two-year-old Golden retriever, appeared quite pleased with herself as she led the way home. After twenty minutes of jockeying for position with the dogs in her neighborhood walking group, Penny had finally taken the lead—courtesy of an intoxicating aroma at the base of a mailbox, which the other four dogs could not resist. Taking advantage of their distraction, Penny sprinted forward, pulling her owner, Tracy, with her.

"Penny, slow down," Tracy said laughingly, gripping the leash with both hands and running to keep up.

But Penny would not relent. She was determination on four paws.

The rest of the group chuckled as Penny dragged Tracy farther and farther ahead of the group.

Penny didn't turn back. She didn't stop. She was on a mission to stay in the lead. And she did.

Not once did she pause to smell the grass, pick up a stick, or mark where she had been. While the other dogs played among themselves, and their humans enjoyed the first coolfront of the year, Penny kept her gaze straight ahead.

Eventually, whether from fatigue or an abundance of confidence, Penny slowed her pace. Tracy took the opportunity to catch her breath and snap a photo of her dog, who was now walking with a distinct swagger.

Tracy knew the photo would be a hit on social media. She typed up a quick caption and hit *share*.

But her joy was short-lived. While Penny stopped to sniff a patch of weeds, Tracy quickly scrolled through the posts on her phone. As she read all the things that others had proudly posted and shared, she was overcome with feelings of failure.

Why can't *I* plan a week's worth of menus for my family?

When was the last time *I* went to the gym?

How does everyone else seem to have it all together?

Then, as if a mental avalanche had been triggered, every item on her ever-expanding to-do list came rushing into her consciousness—a work deadline, costumes to pick up for her kids, a plethora of unread emails in her inbox.

"Ugh, why did I come out today?" Tracy lamented. "I am going to be so far behind."

As Tracy contemplated abandoning the group and running home to try to salvage the rest of her day, she was pulled out of her thoughts when Penny abruptly wheeled around. She braced her front legs against the asphalt and raised her ears in surprise. Penny seemed genuinely shocked to find the others there.

In her determination to get ahead, she had forgotten about those behind.

Melinda, one of the neighbors walking that day, noticed Penny's reaction.

"Penny, when you are leading, you can't forget about your pack," she gently chided the dog.

Melinda's words were meant to tease Penny, but they felt like a lifeline to Tracy. A way to escape the avalanche of to-dos. An anchor in the flood of her feelings of inadequacy.

Tracy did have things to do, but nothing needed to be completed that very moment. Right now, she was part of a pack—a pack committed to encouraging and supporting one another.

Tracy tugged on Penny's leash to get her to take a few steps back. It was all the encouragement the gregarious dog needed to reunite with her friends.

As Penny and her best friend, Layla, leapt toward each other like two polar bears hugging, Tracy tucked her phone into her pocket.

"So, Melinda," she asked the woman walking next to her, whose sister was facing a cancer scare. "How's your sister? And how are you holding up?"

It felt so good to focus on her pack.

PAWS & PONDER . . .

Who is your pack? Are you walking with them? Or charging ahead? In what areas of your life might you need to slow down and remember those who want to walk with you? What is one thing you can do today to remind yourself to slow down and to care for those you are fighting so hard to lead?

Paws & Pray

Father, it is easy to forget about those around me. Even when those around me are family and friends. Would you help me to lead from a place of compassion and rest? Help me to know when to push hard and when to fall back. And as you call me to lead, help me remember and care for those who follow.

100

ᛒEST ᛒAW ᛒORWARD

Do your best, prepare for the worst—then trust God to bring victory.

PROVERBS 21:31, MSG

THE FIRST TIME PHIL AND BONNE saw a Glen of Imaal terrier, a rare Irish dog breed, they were smitten. "It looks like an Irish wolfhound puppy," Phil said.

"I can't believe how laid-back he is. Are you sure this is a terrier?" Bonne asked the owner.

Soon, the couple was picking out a roly-poly puppy and began narrowing down possible names to the final choice: Flurry.

Flurry came with an impressive pedigree—a long line of dog champions on both sides of his family tree. But it was his loving personality that captured their hearts. He seemed to enjoy everyone and everything in the world.

Before long, Phil started training Flurry in dog agility. He wasn't the fastest dog on the course, but he loved the canine playground with its jumps, A-frame, teeter, balance beam, tunnels, and weave poles. But there were other things Phil and Flurry wanted to experience together.

Flurry was certified as a therapy dog, aced obedience training, did rally obedience, and was an engaging representative for the breed at many canine events.

Friends with other Glens encouraged Phil and Bonne to consider entering Flurry in conformation competition with the American Rare Breed Association (ARBA).

A show dog? Flurry's appearance did impress people, but he was used to doing more than walking around a ring or standing still to be examined by a judge.

"What do you think?" Phil asked Bonne.

"Take some classes in conformation and see how Flurry feels about it."

Well . . . Flurry *loved* being in the ring. He could be asleep in his crate, but when it was time to go, he was on—immediately. He was a jaunty showman, playing to the crowd. The only things missing were a top hat and cane.

Flurry was entered in ARBA shows, with Phil and Flurry teaming up in the ring and Bonne serving as driver, roadie, snack-provider, and ad hoc groomer. Thankfully, a Glen is supposed to be scruffy-looking.

Since ARBA was in its early years, most of the shows took place in small venues held in dog exercise areas at hotels or in forest preserves. Flurry nearly always took best of breed honors and was also competitive at the terrier group level.

And then came the exciting news: ARBA was hosting a show in a major city. More than forty of the uncommon dog breeds would be there. Flurry was registered to be one of them.

The metropolitan arena was a far cry from the small outdoor show locations. It was big, loud, and nerve-racking. Phil, Bonne, and Flurry went up and down the rows of dogs, looking for their spot in the staging area. Once they unloaded their gear, they scouted out where their first judging ring was located.

Flurry won handily against the other Glen contenders. The terrier group competition was next—with a Jagdterrier, two Cesky terriers, and Flurry. In conformation, a dog is judged on how well it represents its specific breed standards, not how it compares to its competitors.

At this level, many dogs had professional handlers, or their owners had years of show experience. Phil took a deep breath to relax.

"We've got this, Flur."

"Just do what the two of you have always done," Bonne said.

When Phil entered the ring, the kind judge directed him where to go and what to do. Then the judge put the other three terriers through their paces.

"Will all of you please go around the ring once more?" he instructed when everyone had finished.

When they lined up again, the judge slowly walked alongside them, then stopped. With a slight hand gesture, he quietly called out the final order: "One, two, three, four."

The owner of one of the other terriers had tightened up on his dog's leash and began to take a few steps forward to claim first.

"No, not you—him," the judge said, looking at Flurry.

The person immediately took issue with the judge's decision.

"Why did you choose that dog over mine?"

The judge didn't hesitate. "Because I like his looks. He meets the standards of his breed extremely well."

The challenger wasn't satisfied. "Don't you have to be a champion already, in order to win group?"

As Phil kept Flurry focused, he heard the judge say to the fuming runner-up, "Glens are so rare, there are far fewer opportunities to secure a championship before performing at this level. I think we should let everyone have a chance to play, don't you think?"

The owner scowled, muttered under his breath, and tugged his dog back in line.

Phil and Flurry went on to represent the terrier group in best of show, the one and only time they made it that far. They didn't win, but Phil was pleased. They had accomplished what he had set out to do: give Flurry a chance to show everyone his very best.

PAWS & PONDER...

Whatever battle, situation, or deadline you are facing today, God desires to give you victory—but his victory might look different from what you desire. Are you willing to trust him with the victory? Are you willing to try your best and then surrender the results to him?

Paws & Pray

Father, it is so hard for me to surrender my battles, victories, and results to you. Instead of loosening my grip on things I can't control, I often try to hold on tighter. Forgive me, Lord, and help me to trust you more each day. In the difficult situation I am facing today, help me to prepare and bring my best effort, and then enable me to surrender the results to you—trusting that the victory you have planned for me is the only victory I truly need.

Acknowledgments

THIS BOOK WOULD NOT EXIST without the help of so many people. From my team at Tyndale who not only believed in this book, but also shared their stories with me; to each and every person who submitted a story; to my precious family who endured countless dinners of peanut butter and jelly sandwiches and piles of dirty laundry while *Pawverbs* was being written; to my friends who prayed with me during the writing process and made me believe I could actually write another book . . . thank you. It really does take a village to raise a book baby, and I am so thankful for the village God has given me.

Darrell, you have always believed I can do far more than I ever think I can. Thank you for believing in me all these years and for helping me to believe in myself. You are the love of my life and my best friend, and I am forever grateful to you!

Andrew, once upon a time I was terrified of having a teenager. And then you became one. Buddy, you are the most amazing young man I have ever known. I am so proud to be your mom. The way you love our animals is such a great example of the loving, kind, and overall awesome guy you are! I love you so much and am so excited to have a front-row seat as you begin a new chapter in your life. You've got this, bud, just like you've always got us.

Ella, you bring such sunshine into our lives. It is an honor to be your mom. You shine the love of Jesus into the lives of everyone you meet, and it is beautiful to see. I pray you will always know and believe how very loved and talented you are. Thank you for being such a loving friend and patient teacher to our animal crew. They adore you almost as much as your daddy, brother, and I do. I love you to "English" and back, sweet girl.

Mom and Daddy, there is simply not enough room at the back of a book to express the gratitude that fills my heart when I think of you. Thank you for loving me in such a way that made it easy for me to believe in God's love. Thank you for always believing in me. Thank you for teaching me that when God is in something, nothing can stop it from happening. And thank you for allowing me to have pet grasshoppers, slightly psychotic bunnies, squirrel-killing stray cats, and a long-distance dog! Who could have seen where that was going to lead!

Aunt Judy, you have been my devoted cheerleader/counselor. Knowing I could pick up the phone anytime to celebrate with you, cry with you, or just process something with you made this book so much easier to write. I see so much of Grandmother in you. You truly are such a gift, and I am so very grateful for you. I pray you always know and believe how loved and valued you are.

Sarah Atkinson, if you and Jan Long Harris hadn't stopped by Hope Reins that hot August day, *Pawverbs* would still just be a fun title for a collection of stories I made up for my kids. Thank you for hearing and seeing something in my idea when I did not.

Bonne Steffen, you are so much more than an editor to me. You are a mentor, a teacher, and a friend. One of God's greatest gifts to me in this writing journey was allowing me to work with and learn from you. Thank you for everything you have done to bring this book to life. I truly believe the entire editorial team should wear superhero capes because that is what you all are!

Carol Traver, now that the book is done I'm going to have to think of other reasons to call you so I can hear more Sephy stories! Thank you for sharing your kitties—and your heart—with me. It has been an honor. I pray their stories bring you joy and help others see a glimpse of God's own heart.

And to Kara Leonino, Jackie Nunez, Babette Rea, Jillian Schlossberg,

Kristen Magnesen, Andrea Martin, Dean Renninger, Ron Kaufmann, Katie Dodillet, Cassidy Gage, and Maria Eriksen, thank you so very much for making me feel a part of the Tyndale family, for sharing stories with me, and for supporting this project. You all are such a gift.

To Jessica Kirkland, my amazing agent and friend. I don't think I can ever thank you enough for taking my phone call that day. How could we have ever known where that call would lead? I am forever grateful to you for helping me chase dreams. You are a gem of a human being and I am honored to know you.

To Honnie Korngold, thank you for your constant encouragement and support. You are such a gift to this world, and I am so excited to see what God has in store! Thank you for your commitment to tell stories full of hope and light.

To those who allowed me to share their stories: Deputy Field Cross, April Kolstad, Nancy Self, Vicky Giesgh, Amy Sorrells, Nicole Ball, Kathy Brown, Caitlyn Hawkins, Eileen Brown, Ronda Haslemayer, Brenda McLamb, Patti Chriestenson, Joe Hawley, Karen Wellman, Crystal Kranz, Amy Harris, Mollie Johnson, Emily Potter, Karen Stofer, Sergeant Brandon Cox, Sandee Thomas, Ken and Janet Slagle, Crystal Sides, Marie Blanton, Paul Batura, Bethany Russell, Marie Kirby, Caroline Hunt, Bonnie Glueck, Judith Hoffman, Nancy Beckmann, Lindy Williams, Cat Jones, Barbara Moranta, Sarah Thompson, and Donna Ols.

Thank you for trusting me with your stories and for sharing your animal babies with me. I pray this book honors the animals you love. And for those whose animal is no longer with you, I pray this book will honor their memory and that their lives will impact others for years to come. It was a joy to talk and interact with each and every one of you. I am forever grateful for your generosity.

And to my precious friends who prayed for me, shared stories with me, helped me remember stories, and kept calling and texting me while I retreated into my writing hole—thank you. I could not have written this book without your support and love. I am so grateful for each and every one of you.

Let love and faithfulness never leave you;

bind them around your neck,

write them on the tablet of your heart.

PROVERBS 3:3, NIV

About the Author

JENNIFER BLEAKLEY is the author of *Joey: How a Blind Rescue Horse Helped Others Learn to See*; a former child and family grief counselor; and a children's curriculum writer. When Jennifer is not typing away on her beat-up computer, you can find her spending time with her talented software engineer/woodworking husband, her two growing children, and her very needy Golden retriever. She and her family live in Raleigh, North Carolina.

A heartwarming true story of

LOYALTY, KINDNESS & HEALING,

Joey is a profound testament to the power of blind faith.

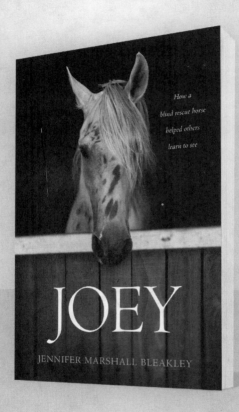

When a struggling ranch owner dedicated to helping troubled kids rescues a blind horse named Joey, the result is a story of friendship, faith, and overcoming. *Joey* will touch your heart and reveal the power of finding light in the darkest of places.

Also available from Tyndale House Publishers

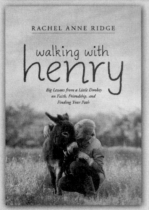

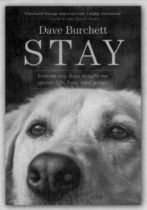